MODERN FENCING

MICHEL ALAUX
U.S. Olympic Fencing Coach

MODERN FENCING

FOIL
EPEE
SABRE
from Initiation to Competition

CHARLES SCRIBNER'S SONS   New York

Library of Congress Cataloging in Publication Data

Alaux, Michel.
    Modern fencing.

    1. Fencing. I. Title.
    GV1147.A42   796.8′6   74–30128
    ISBN 0–684–14116–7

1 3 5 7 9 11 13 15 17 19 C/H 20 18 16 14 12 10 8 6 4 2

Printed in the United States of America

CONTENTS

ELECTRICAL APPARATUS 168

LESSONS 171

CONDITIONING 180
with Marius Valsamis, M.D., Associate Professor of Pathology at Albert Einstein Medical School

PREFACE

Michel Alaux, who wrote this book, was Maître d'Armes at the Fencers Club in New York, thrice a coach of the United States Olympic Fencing Team, master of World and Olympic Champion Christian d'Oriola, responsible for the national men's and women's foil individual and team champions, for national epee champions, and others. These are impressive credentials (and there are more, including decorations from his native France of the Gold Medal of Honor, the highest decoration awarded by the French Minister of Sports, which was followed in 1962 by the "Academic Palms," awarded for services rendered to sports by the French Minister of Education). This book is a testimony to Alaux's credentials, a history that traces the fusion of nationally originated techniques into an international style.

A long road has been traveled since Nicolas Demeuse, "Garde-du-Corps de S.A.C. le Prince-Evêque de Liège et Maître en Fait-d'Armes," wrote his *Nouveau Traité de l'Art des Armes* in 1668. He begins with the "salut," requiring that the left hand, slowly and gracefully, lift one's hat, without moving the head, and looking respectfully, straight at the master! It would be a rare salle d'armes, indeed, where these formalities are still observed. Yet a salute at the beginning, courtesy during the bout, and the thanks and handshake at the end are more than vestigial remnants.

Modern competitive fencing requires physical conditioning perhaps to a greater extent than in earlier years. At the Fencers Club, where Alaux presided, this is seen in the emphasis on warmup, pre-lesson calisthenics, and general muscle tone through both group and individual exercises and footwork. All this is reflected in this book, which nevertheless is concerned with the preeminence of the mental, psychological, and intellectual requirements that help to make a champion fencer.

The chapter on "Lessons" is a revealing insight into the problems the master faces in teaching beginners, champions, and the non-competitor group. In this area, Michel Alaux was indeed the master. I have alluded to some of the products of his skills, and those of us who had lessons from him know how soundly his reputation is based.

Michel came to the Fencers Club in 1956 after having established himself in his own salle in Montpellier in France. He is a graduate of the French Military School of Fencing and Combat Sports in Antibes, which after World War II succeeded the prestigious College of Physical Education of Joinville le Pont. In his salle, he established the foundations for his career in the United States, which began when he replaced the renowned René Pinchart, who had been master at the Fencers Club since 1924. Alaux made the difficult adjustments always required of a replacement and stood at the pinnacle of his profession when he died unexpectedly this year.

1975   Eugene Blanc, Jr.
                                              PRESIDENT, NEW YORK FENCERS CLUB

ACKNOWLEDGMENTS

Although fencing masters are like other professional men and hope to crown their careers by finding a publisher for the memoires of their years of experience, it never occurred to me that some day I would be fortunate enough to be sought out to write a book on fencing. The challenge was placed squarely on my shoulders when Patricia Cristol asked me to present fencing under a different aspect from the one usually followed in fencing books but without eliminating the very purpose of setting forth the technique of fencing. I tried, therefore, to do something which could interest not only fencers, but people not initiated to our sport.

My dear student and friend Averil Genton did not know what was ahead when she proposed to type the manuscript for me. She accepted all the many changes while learning to decipher my handwriting with the same stoicism she manifests when taking fencing lessons from me. My deep gratitude goes to her for her patience and high professional standard in doing a difficult job.

How I managed to write a book while involved with the everyday task of making a living teaching fencing is as much a surprise to me now that the book is at the printing stage as it is to Eugene Blanc, who willingly accepted the task of writing the preface, for which I am very thankful.

No individual goes through life without developing a hobby, which for some may be related to their field of activity but for most is totally unrelated to their daily chores. I found out that trout fishing and fencing have much in common, if only for the concentration and mental state of readiness needed to make the "strike" at the proper moment. I have spent many hours wading in the beautiful streams of New York State and Massachusetts in search of the evasive trout with my pupils James Melcher, twice National Epee Champion, his lovely wife, Barbara, and Ruth White, twice National Women's Foil Champion, who exhibits as much determination in catching the most fish as she does in winning fencing competitions. I have also enjoyed the company of my friend Dr. Marius Valsamis, a recent convert to fishing. Their help in writing this book and providing me with the opportunity to relax from it all has been invaluable.

MODERN FENCING

INTRODUCTION

For many people fencing represents a romantic attachment to the past, a past in which swashbuckling heroes abound—heroes whose adventures and prowess have been portrayed so vividly in such movies as *The Three Musketeers* and *Cyrano de Bergerac*. For some, fencing is a kind of mysterious religion practiced by a "coterie" whose members deal with rapier or dueling sword. The thought of belonging tempts and frightens them both, bringing about an ambivalence of emotion: the fear to relive the bloody fighting of the past and a desire to learn the secrets of its pageantry.

For most fencers, fencing is a unique combination of quick thinking and elegant athletic movements. Whatever the reasons for taking up this sport, those who do will enjoy a combat sport that, unlike boxing or wrestling, does not require body contact but rather the use of a weapon. Pure strength, although not useless, loses its intrinsic value against the more efficient element of physical and mental reflexes. These reflexes are intimately involved in giving the fencer the kind of balance that will allow him to react at a speed that makes fencing action barely visible on a television screen. At the time of action, a fencer has 1/20th of a second to think up a proper move and 1/20th of a second to carry on the action. The demand for instant analysis, decision making, and speed in carrying out the action require almost computerlike response from the mind.

Once a fencer has learned the mechanics of basic fencing movements, the activity loses its primary total physical requirement and becomes more of a mental exercise. Concentration, self-control, and a quick decision command muscles and reflexes for a successful scoring.

It has often been said that fencing is a physical chess game. This is not to say that fencing does not require, maintain, or develop physical ability and conditioning. Both have a bearing on the degree of proficiency one may be able to reach. However, success depends to a great extent on the fencer's ability to deal with his opponent's game: to annihilate his strongest points as well as to take advantage of his weaknesses. In other words, technique and tactics are the main component of the sport of fencing.

There are no prerequisites for learning fencing, developing its technique, or reaching a championship level. However, anyone wishing to learn fencing—whether interested in physical activity and striving for perfection or wishing to become a top competitor—will find that fencing involves total participation of mind and body.

In past centuries, fencing was a basic part of the education of every nobleman in Europe. Although its purpose was survival, the development of character and mental qualities through the practice of fencing was not overlooked. In many European schools fencing is still very much a part of the curriculum and in the United States it is found more and more often among the extracurricular activities of many high schools and colleges.

The educational aspect of the sport has been somewhat forgotten with the development of professionalism and the athletic requirements of the modern Olympic Games. However, while professionalism has its place, it concerns only a small percentage of talented athletes. Sports as a part of education should be emphasized more for its moral and physical health aspects.

Fencing, unlike many other sports, requires relatively little in equipment and practice space and yet produces so many beneficial effects. Age is not a factor. Indeed, many fencers over seventy are still practicing regularly and it is not unusual to see teenagers competing with adults of all ages. To paraphrase General MacArthur's famous remark about old soldiers: "Old fencers never die, they simply fade away."

In our stressful society there is a great need to rediscover the beneficial effects of individual sports, and fencing is one of the most rewarding.

HISTORY OF FENCING

Since the cave man first fashioned a club, men have invented weapons to defend themselves either to protect against animals and other human beings or to conquer them. From stone ax to dueling sword, weapons have been transformed and evolved. Their development has followed patterns that reflect the values of the social, artistic, and technological development of various cultures.

In the highly developed civilizations of Greece and Rome, short swords, light spears, and shields were used. With the fall of the Roman Empire (about A.D. 476) until the fourteenth century, weapons became heavier and more cumbersome, reflecting a regression to all areas of social and cultural life. Brute force, violence, and cruelty in fighting were the predominant characteristics of this period, when heavy armor, coats of mail, two-handed swords, and heavy halberds (a spear and ax combined on a long pole) prevailed. The need for swift weapons with sharp points to penetrate between the joints of armor led to the development of the rapier. Then in the fourteenth century, the appearance of gunpowder made armor ineffective.

Although fencing schools may have developed much earlier in India (mention is made in sacred books of Brahmans teaching fencing in public places), it appears that modern fencing was born in Spain, where the first

3

books on fencing were published by Sierge de Valera in 1471 and by two Spanish fencing masters, Pons from Perpignan and Pedro de Torre, in 1474.

After the Renaissance duelists spent most of their time trying to discover the "botte secret" and "universal parry," and the rapier became a decorative ornament for dress. In the sixteenth century, Italian fencing masters were predominant and the most popular in Europe. They were also prolific publishers of fencing manuals.

Agrippa in 1553 described the first four fencing positions (prime, seconde, tierce, and quarte) and recommended the use of the point thrust to the opponent's face, instead of to the body, which was protected by a coat of mail. Grassi and Vigiani (1575) described the lunge. (Fencing terms like "thrust" and "lunge" and the various positions are explained in detail later in this book.)

Under Catherine de Médicis, Queen of France, and of Italian heritage, Italian fencing masters were in demand in France and helped develop fencing in that country. Associations of fencing masters were already in existence in Germany, and England also had an association of fencers.

In 1567, the French Fencing Academy was recognized by "lettre de patente" of King Charles IX (Catherine de Médicis' son) and confirmed by his royal successors until the Revolution of 1789. To express the high esteem in which the king held the profession of fencing master, he ennobled a certain number of masters with hereditary titles.

The French fencing masters became the first to define the principles of fencing and to develop a methodical classification of attacks and parries (defensive movements that deflect attacks). The first treatise by a French fencing master, Henry de St. Didier, was published in 1573. He advocated the use of the epee without the dagger for both offense and defense. However, the dagger was used until the seventeenth century.

Dueling was very popular during the sixteenth century. In fact so many noblemen were killed in these encounters that both the king of France and the queen of England banned dueling. The edict, however, had very little or no effect in reducing the number of people killed. More noblemen were dying in duels than in war.

In the middle of the seventeenth century, the "colichemarde" replaced the rapier. Its blade, thinner and sharper at the tip, favored actions with the point. Fencing flourished all over Europe. The "real" Cyrano de Bergerac took lessons from a famous French fencing master, La Perce du Coudray.

French and Italian fencing schools had already developed their own characteristics. Around 1650, the "fioretta" (Italian for flower), called "fleuret" in French and "foil" in English, became the training weapon for dueling and accentuated the difference between the two schools. In the eighteenth century, the small sword with its triangular blade (similar to the one used in epee today) became the weapon for dueling, while the sabre became the national weapon of Hungary.

The invention of the mask, before the French Revolution, by a French fencing master, La Boissière, helped establish the definitive foundation of our modern fencing with its present en-garde ("on-guard") position and technique.

In Germany, dueling among students was very popular and fencing was practiced with a "schlager." Its blade was large, with no point but a sharp edge. Only blows at the cheeks were allowed, the rest of the body being safely protected by heavy leather clothing. Dueling was performed while standing still, at weapon's distance from the head. Students displayed scars on their cheeks as a mark of courage; this custom existed until the Second World War.

Russia had a few French fencing masters during the reign of the czars. The most prominent, A. Grisier, spent ten years teaching Russian princes and noblemen of the imperial court. He dedicated his book, *Les Armes et le Duel,* to his Imperial Majesty, Nicholas I. His book was prefaced by Alexandre Dumas, who wrote *The Three Musketeers.* However, from the time of the Russian Revolution until the Second World War, fencing was considered a "bourgeois" sport and completely disappeared in Russia. French and Italian masters displayed their talent throughout the world. By the end of the nineteenth century, some went to America and were responsible for the development of fencing in the United States.

With the suppression of dueling and the organization of the Olympic Games (Athens, Greece, in 1896), fencing developed into a popular sport. Italian, French, and Hungarian fencers dominated international fencing tournaments until 1956. As fencing became more popular in countries not previously represented in international competition—particularly behind the Iron Curtain—Poland, Romania, and the Soviet Union became strong contenders for Olympic and World Championship titles.

The Soviet Union's first participation in competition was in 1946. In the 1968 Olympics, held in Mexico City, the Soviet Union garnered three gold medals and four silver medals, thereby accumulating the greatest number of points in the fencing events. Behind the success of Soviet fencers was government subsidy and organizational support.

For a considerable period prior to the emergence of the Soviet Union, Poland, Hungary, and Romania as dominant fencing powers, the French and Italian fencing techniques prevailed. Each had its own characteristics based on different hand grips as well as on the temperaments of each country.

The French handle is reasonably thick, to allow for point control with finger action. The Italian handle provides a cross bar across the handle and often requires attachment by a leather strap around the wrist. The French temperament made for finesse by using simple, fine, point actions, while the Italian temperament called for aggressive and powerful attacks on the blade coupled with fast footwork. With improvement in technique and physical conditioning and the trend toward use of the French handle, the two schools of fencing tended to fuse into an international technique combining the elements of both styles.

In present-day fencing competition, it would be difficult to recognize the product of any particular school or technique. A fencer develops a personal style that mainly reflects the teaching of his fencing master rather than any national school. The modern successful fencing master develops the basic natural qualities of a prospective fencing champion instead of following a rigidly standardized instruction technique.

JEAN-LOUIS MICHEL

Fencing is rich in "épopées." Its traditions have been transmitted through generations and are still honored. Saluting the opponent before and after a bout, accepting the decision of the jury with good grace, following the rules and conventions of the game, behaving with the manners of a gentleman, accepting defeat as well as victory with graciousness make fencing a truly educational sport.

The Three Musketeers may have been fictitious and the product of a fertile mind, but many episodes as dramatic as those included in the book have occurred in real life. Such is the case of "Jean-Louis," who was born in 1785 on the Island of St. Domingue, now the Republic of Haiti. Before I arrived in the United States I was fortunate to have been for eight years the fencing master of a very old fencing club called Association Jean-Louis in the French city of Montpellier. The club was named after its founder, "Jean-Louis," who came to Montpellier in 1830.

Since then, the club has been an important fencing center in France and produced world and Olympic champions. Unfortunately, the association had to be dissolved shortly after my departure for the United States. Jean-Louis' life story through the diplomas and awards he gathered during his lifetime has been preserved and can be read on the walls of the club as part of the heritage left to his successors. I felt that in a book on fencing a short history of Jean-Louis would be of some interest.

The island of St. Domingue had been one of France's colonies since 1697, when Spain ceded it to the French, and was still a colony during the period of the French Revolution. Its inhabitants, mostly blacks, were descendants of slaves brought there from Africa. Although some insurrections had taken place before, it was not until 1795, under the leadership of Toussaint L'Ouverture, that the black population of the island succeeded in gaining its independence by defeating a French expeditionary army led by General Leclerc.

The island became the Republic of Haiti in 1804. During the insurrection of 1795 many Haitians, particularly mulattoes, took advantage of a decree from the French National Assembly to emigrate to France. They were mostly military men anxious to avoid the repression of the black population.

Among those who emigrated to France were General Dumas, father of the famous French writer Alexandre Dumas, author of *The Three Musketeers,* and a young mulatto, eleven years old, traveling alone. He was a puny, thin little boy who wanted to become a soldier in the French army.

His appearance was such that when he arrived at the French military school, the colonel in charge asked, "Who the devil has had the genial idea to accept this 'avorton'?" A sergeant told him that Jean-Louis Michel was an orphan who had come from the island of St. Domingue just a few months ago. Touched by his situation, the colonel allowed the youngster to stay and sent him to the fencing master to give him an opportunity to develop physically, although doubting that he would become a soldier.

Mistakenly, the colonel called Michel by his first name, Jean-Louis, which was to remain his last name until his death. The fencing master D'Erapes, a titled man of Belgian origin (Belgium was conquered by France in 1795), took Jean-Michel under his tutelage. The prévôts (assistants to the fencing master) did not show much compassion or understanding or willingness to help Jean-Louis. On the contrary, they constantly made jokes about his color and physical appearance.

Jean-Louis faced the situation with great stoicism for a boy his age, neither answering the provocations nor getting discouraged. He spent most of his time at the salle d'armes, observing intently, particularly when the fencing master was giving lessons. When alone, he drilled himself on the different actions taught by the fencing master during the lessons.

One day D'Erapes, having noticed Jean-Louis' determination and dedication, decided to give him lessons. Highly impressed by his form, speed, and self-control, he helped and encouraged him, and Jean-Louis soon became a model of execution. Applying the same determination when bouting with the best fencers of the regiment, it did not take too long for him to develop into a formidable fencer.

Every year, a fencing demonstration was given by the best fencers before the entire regiment. It was quite an honor for those selected, and one year Jean-Louis became one of them. A few years later, he took his examination for fencing master before the finest jury ever assembled, which included the best duelists and fencing masters from all over the country. He passed with honors, and highest praises were given him for his knowledge and ability. He was the youngest candidate ever presented.

With his regiment Jean-Louis took part in most military campaigns during the Napoleonic era. He participated in more than thirty battles, including the Egyptian campaign and the Spanish War. Promoted to "Tambour Major," he was always in front of his brigade while charging the enemy.

Although Napoleon was against dueling—a rather strange attitude for a man who conquered Europe through continuous wars—pride and an intense sense of honor caused many deadly encounters between soldiers. Jean-Louis had his share of successful duels and was considered the finest blade in the army. Very popular among both soldiers and high-ranking officers, he used his amazing fencing ability with restraint.

One day a military man made an unsavory remark about Jean-Louis' bravery, adding, "All these foils would do very little in front of a real weapon." Jean-Louis decided to give a lesson to the "bravache." "I accept your challenge," he said, "on one condition—that you fence with your dueling weapon and I with my foil." Without any qualms, Jean-Louis' opponent acquiesced to the condition and the duel took place.

They faced each other, and after a few minutes of observation and quick exchanges, Jean-Louis parried his opponent's attack while retreating, and followed with another strong parry, which immobilized the opponent's weapon. Then, releasing his hold suddenly, Jean-Louis slashed his foe's face with a mighty swing of his foil blade. This unusual riposte ended all belligerence on the part of Jean-Louis' opponent, who for a long time kept the wound and the memory of his duel with Jean-Louis.

During the Spanish War many regiments made up of different nationalities were taking part in the battles. The 32nd Regiment was one of them. The campaign was not too successful. Spirit was low among soldiers, leading to many quarrels that ended in duels.

Death in duels became so prevalent that soon whole regiments became involved. One day, more than a hundred men of an Italian and a French regiment found themselves involved in an argument and were ready to slaughter each other, but the massacre was averted. However, army discipline required that reparation be made between the two regiments. The general in charge decided that fifteen fencing masters and prévôts from each regiment would fight in duels. All these men were experienced and highly trained. Used to facing death every day without fear, they were determined to defend the honor of the regiment they represented at the cost of their lives.

The duels took place in a wide-open field around Madrid. In the center of the field was an empty space forming a sort of natural platform that served as the dueling strip. The two regiments were placed in battle formation around the field, every one of the ten thousand men watching intently. Among the French fencing masters, Jean-Louis was the first to be in line. His opponent was Giacomo Ferrari, a redoubtable fencing master from the 1st Italian Regiment.

As soon as the command to fight was given, Giacomo attacked savagely with a crushing thrust. Jean-Louis parried and held for a while to control his opponent's blade, then riposted with lightning speed, wounding Giacomo in the shoulder. The latter got up screaming, "It's nothing, start the fight again." The duel started again, but this time Jean-Louis' epee entered deeply and Giacomo was dead. Jean-Louis wiped the blood from his weapon and waited for the next opponent. The winner was supposed to fight again and meet the next opponent unless wounded or incapacitated.

Jean-Louis faced his second opponent. After a few minutes of blade play, Jean-Louis lunged and while recovering left his point in line. His opponent mistakenly attacked at that time and went into Jean-Louis' point, which entered his body deeply, killing him instantly. Among screams and shouting from the soldiers, the next opponent and the next suffered the same fate, being wounded or killed, until the thirteenth one fell unconscious.

In forty minutes and twenty-seven strokes only two Italian provosts were left. A truce was called and the colonel of the 32nd Regiment approached Jean-Louis. "Maître, you have valiantly defended the regiment's honor and in the name of your comrades and my name, I thank you sincerely. However, thirteen consecutive duels have taken too much of your body stamina. Retire now and if the provosts decide to finish the combat with their opponents, they will be free to do so." "No!" Jean-Louis exploded. "I will not leave without fulfilling my duty. I will stay as long as I can hold my weapon." While saying these words, Jean-Louis made a gesture and in the excitement wounded one of his friends on the leg. "Ah," cried out Jean-Louis, "there is only one man of the 32nd Regiment who has been wounded, and it had to be with my weapon."

The colonel took advantage of the incident and told Jean-Louis, "This is a warning; there has been enough blood. All have fought bravely and reparation has been made. Do you trust my judgment in the matter of honor?" "Yes, colonel," answered Jean-Louis. "Then I declare that honor is satisfied and that the 32nd Regiment has only one thing to do—extend a loyal hand to the 1st Regiment." The two Italian provosts remaining were silent and waiting. The colonel pointed them out to Jean-Louis and said, "They cannot come to you personally." Jean-Louis, subdued, finally threw away his weapon and with fear in his eyes stretched a friendly hand toward the two Italians.

The two regiments, aware of the dramatic situation, let out a roaring shout, "Long live the Thirty-second Regiment!" Jean-Louis replied, "Long live the First Regiment; we are all again one and from the same family. Long live the army."

Jean-Louis was then twenty-eight years old and his reputation was at its zenith. He refused a promotion to officer so that he did not have to renounce his position as fencing master. But he was awarded the highest decoration of the "Legion of Honor" at the age of twenty-nine. Later he received the "Medaille de St. Hélène" bestowed by Napoleon from his prisoner's island to his faithful soldiers and followers. In 1816 Jean-Louis was the fencing master of the 32nd Regiment of the Engineers Corps in Montpellier, a charming little town in the south of France.

The return of the nobility after the fall of Napoleon, newly rich people trying to emulate the nobles, and jealousies and quarrels among factions gave this town a very special atmosphere. All this very well served the personality of Jean-Louis, who attempted to unite people rather than lead them into duels. He was consulted in all matters pertaining to honor and to the city's administration. He left Montpellier for a town in the north of France, Metz, where he opened a very successful salle d'armes.

In 1820, during the "Restauration," fencing assumed an important place in the educational system and was extremely popular, as were duels. Jean-Louis was quoted as saying, "The blood of a soldier must not be wasted stupidly. The duel is an end. The purpose of fencing consists more to calm down the excess of passion through consciousness of one's strength and sentiment of superiority that one acquires than trying to hit the opponent. The purpose of fencing is also to develop a man with enough self-control so as to make him able to direct his attack with accuracy and avoid as much as possible the deadly end."

Jean-Louis was looked upon as one of the best judges and referees in fencing matches and duels. However, he never agreed to referee a duel without trying to convince the opponents that excuses would be sufficient in the pending matter. He directed some of the most famous and spectacular fencing bouts of the period. One of the most memorable was in 1816 between the Comte de Bondy, who was then prefect (governor of state) of the Seine Department, and Lafaugere, one of the greatest fencing masters ever to live. The count considered himself the best fencer of the period and could not stand the idea of anybody being superior to him. He showed so much disdain for Lafaugere's reputation that the Comte D'Ivry arranged a public bout between the two at the Quai D'Orsay, one of the most imposing buildings in Paris.

The jury was made up of the best amateurs and fencing masters of France and was presided over by Jean-Louis. The large room could not contain sufficient seats for all the spectators present, who included some of the most important people politically and socially. When the two fencers appeared on the strip, the tall count was wearing a magnificent jacket made of white satin with a frill of fine lace, while Lafaugere was wearing the usual fencing jacket appropriate for this event. Slightly irritated by such an ostentatious appearance on the part of his opponent, Lafaugere could not resist telling the count, "Don't you believe, Monsieur le Comte, that for such a serious bout this costume is a little too delicate?" The count, surprised by the remark, smiled and said, "Not at all, my dear sir. I am used to this jacket and never wear anything else when I have the good fortune to meet a fencer like you."

Jean-Louis, sensing that the conversation could easily turn into a provocation for a duel, asked the fencers to position themselves for the bout. "En garde, Messieurs. Etes-vous pret? Allez!" The fencers engaged their blades while total silence reigned in the room. After five minutes of quick fencing actions, Lafaugere had torn apart the count's fine lace jabot, while the satin jacket itself bore large scratches inflicted by Lafaugere's foil. The bout lasted twenty minutes. The final score was twenty-seven hits against the count and two against Lafaugere. A second bout lasted fifteen minutes. The count was hit twenty-three times, Lafaugere only once! After the bout, unable to stand the humiliation, the count confined himself to bed and did not appear in public for a few days.

Around 1830 Jean-Louis returned to Montpellier and opened a salle d'armes which became famous and one of the most important fencing centers in the country. Jean-Louis was surrounded with admiration and respect and was a public figure in the city. When important personages such as generals or ministers were received by the municipality, he was always the guest of honor at the dinners. In 1834, he married a lovely and devoted lady, Josephine Montes, of Spanish origin. A daughter was born who later married a Doctor Veillard. Under Jean-Louis' tutoring this daughter became a redoubtable fencer equal to many of the best male fencers. She died childless. Her life inspired the writing of an operetta, *The Twenty Days of Pierrette*.

In 1849 Jean-Louis, then sixty-five years old, was again called to solve a serious situation between two regiments stationed in Montpellier, an infantry regiment and a regiment of engineers corps. A great rivalry existed between soldiers of the two regiments. It started with a duel between two men, followed by other duels, until the commandant general of the area was called to Paris by the minister of war to be told that the situation could no longer be tolerated. On his return the general called upon Jean-Louis for a solution to the problem. Jean-Louis decided that the best way to settle the differences between the two regiments was to bring the soldiers together. He organized a fencing competition with fencers from both regiments, while their comrades were to attend as spectators.

Jean-Louis directed every bout and made commentaries that brought laughter and smiles to the soldiers' faces, thus opening the way for a reconciliation. In 1865 Jean-Louis, with both eyes affected by cataracts, became blind. However, he still gave lessons to his old pupils. Aided by his unparalleled feel and control of the blade, he gave his lessons sitting on a chair. He was then eighty-five years old.

Jean-Louis' wife died at the beginning of 1865. They were so close to each other that when she died Jean-Louis told his friends, "My dear friends, I have received a warning; before the year is over, I will be reunited again with my dearest wife." His prediction was accurate. He died in November 1865 and was buried in Montpellier, where his grave is still in the cemetery.

FOIL

EQUIPMENT

Mask and Uniform

Both are safety devices designed to ensure total protection to the fencer against injury. The mask that protects the face and front of the neck is made of steel mesh strong enough to withstand the hardest hit. As a safety measure, the mask has top priority. The fencer should never gamble by using a damaged or rusty mask.

The uniform consists of a jacket and knickers, which must be white and made of strong and resistant material. They should fit the fencer without being too tight so as to allow complete freedom of movement. All fencers in official competition are required to wear a safety inner canvas underarm protector under the jacket, and women must wear breast plates inside their jacket as well. (Pockets are attached on the inner part of the jacket for this purpose.)

The glove is generally made of thin leather or a combination of leather and canvas to protect the fencing hand.

To complete the uniform, the fencer wears long white socks, which protect the legs up to the knee. White tennis or fencing shoes also are worn.

Weapon

Fencing can be practiced with three weapons. Each weapon is made of two basic parts: the *blade* and the *mounting*. The blade is manufactured of steel with different shapes and degrees of flexibility depending on the weapon. Every blade has a strong part (the third of the blade that is near the hand) called "forte"; the next third of the blade is called the "medium";

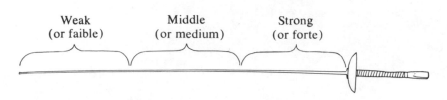

Weak
(or faible)

Middle
(or medium)

Strong
(or forte)

and the part toward the tip is called the "foible," or weak. The blade itself has a narrow section at its base, which is called the "shank." The parts of the mounting are affixed on it.

The foil blade is lighter than the epee blade to allow faster and more complex action. While a stiff blade gives more authority in an action, a light blade is often too "whippy," thus having some bearing on point accuracy. A heavy blade, of course, slows down speed of action. It is essential for competitors to select carefully the type of blade they particularly desire.

The mounting consists of three parts. The "guard," made of light metal, generally aluminum, protects the hand, particularly in epee and sabre. The shape varies with the type of weapon. The guard must be uniformly polished and smooth, without asperity so as not to hinder the opponent's point during the course of a fencing phrase.

The "handle," by which the weapon is held, is usually made of wood wrapped with cord or leather. However, handles of different shape to fit the hand have become very popular. They are pistol-grip handles made of either plastic or aluminum. This type of handle has some advantage over the French handle in that it gives more authority and power during exchanges. However, it tends to accentuate tension in the hand and does not allow as much point control as the French handle does.

The "pommel" is usually made of brass, threaded on the inside so it can be tightened onto the threaded part of the shank of the blade. The pommel has a dual purpose: it holds the various parts of the weapon together, and it serves as a counterweight to the blade, giving a better balance and making the handling of the weapon much easier.

A thumb pad must be inserted between the guard and the handle to prevent the thumb from hitting the guard.

Blades and mountings are generally standard. The weight, shape, and characteristics must comply with norms defined and established by the International Fencing Federation, which represents all national fencing federations in the Olympic Committee.

FENCING STRIP

The strip is the delineated portion of the ground that is used during a bout between two fencers. Any flat surface made of wood, rubber, or linoleum, and so on can be used. However, it is recommended that fencing on extremely hard surfaces such as concrete, or too slippery surfaces such as waxed floors, be avoided to prevent injuries. Wood, because of its suppleness, is most desirable.

Dimensions: The width of the strip is the same for all weapons: 1.80 to 2 meters (5'11" to 6'7") in official competitions. The length for the foil strip is 12 meters (39'4"), while for epee and sabre it is 24 meters (78'9"). However, for practical purposes, the three weapons are fenced on the same strip (that of foil). The additional distances needed in epee and sabre are awarded to the fencer who has reached his own end of the strip by bringing him to the starting line and fencing again as if it were a strip of continuous length.

The strip is divided by lines: the center line, which is in the middle of the strip; the en-garde (or starting) lines, which are 2 meters on either side of the center line; the warning lines, which for foil are at one meter from each end of the strip and at 2 meters from each end of the strip for epee and sabre. Finally, there are the rear lines, which represent the ends of the strip.

The regulation F.I.C. and A.F.L.A. fencing strip

The width of the strip shall be a minimum of 1.8 meters (5'-10") and a maximum of 2 meters (6'-7"). The length of the retreat zone shall be a minimum of 1.8 meters (5'-10") and a maximum of 2 meters (6'-7"). For foil and epee, the metallic surface of the strip shall cover the entire retreat zone.

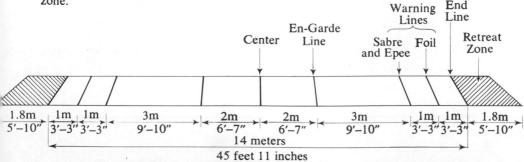

GRIP

This concerns solely the French handle, as any other type of handle provides for a systematic way of holding the weapon. The French handle is made of a section of wood or plastic about seven inches long of quadrangular shape with a curve allowing the handle to fit comfortably in the palm of the hand.

Right-hand grip on French handle

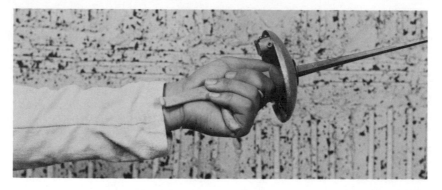

Left-hand grip on pistol handle

To hold the weapon, the lower part of the handle rests on the second phalange (or between the first and second phalange) of the index finger. The thumb is stretched on the opposite side, almost touching the guard, while the other three fingers lie on the handle, not tightly but ready to support the action of the thumb and index.

The role of the thumb and index is extremely important. They control and guide the point. Accuracy depends primarily upon their action; so does the "feeling" of the blade. They act with a kind of pinching motion.

An old fencing master described the grip on the weapon as similar to

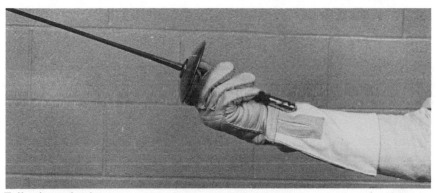

Foil grip supination

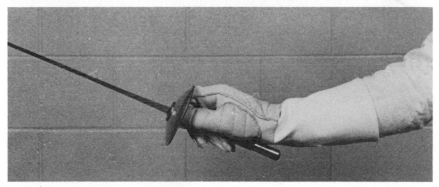

pronation

French, Italian, and pistol grips

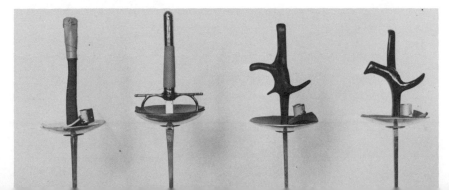

holding a bird in the hand—"Not too tight so as not to smother the bird; not too loose so that it cannot fly away." A firm hold without fingers tightened will avoid fatigue, allow resisting any action of force on the part of the opponent, and allow use of more power whenever it is necessary.

The above grip is recommended as opposed to holding the weapon on the tips of the fingers. The fencer should also avoid holding the weapon with the fingers away from the guard.

The pommel should be maintained on an axis parallel to the forearm. Avoid bending the wrist, which is the tendency of most beginners when trying to keep the hand palm up or the point at eye level.

On the subject of the grip, fencers must take special care to avoid mounting their weapon with the blade coming out straight from the guard. A slight curving (inside and down) should be given to the shank of the blade before assembling the weapon so that the point will not be out of line when the weapon is being properly held.

TARGET

The target in foil consists of that part of the trunk (excluding arms and head) which in front extends upward from the groin lines and in back

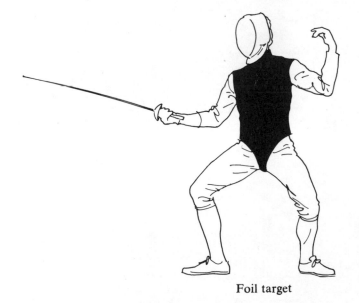

Foil target

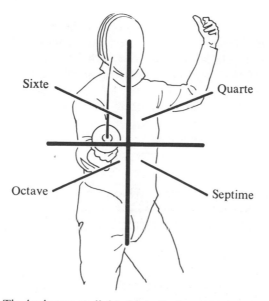

The body target divided into its four quarters

upward from an imaginary horizontal line passing across the top of the hips. The legs, arms, neck, and head are considered "off target," or not valid.

In official competitions in which electrical apparatus is used, a metallic jacket is worn by the fencers. This jacket must conform exactly to the fencer's valid target. Before every competition the dimensions of the jacket are checked on the fencers by the manager of the meet.

LINES

The lines are portions of space delineated by two imaginary lines, one vertical and the other horizontal, which meet at the center of the target area. These lines divide the target into four areas: two high lines and two low lines, or two inside lines and two outside lines.

Each area can be safely protected with a specific blade motion called a *parry*. It can be done by moving the blade laterally or vertically, by moving the hand in supination (hand palm up) or pronation (hand palm down), while executing the defensive move. There are eight possible hand positions (two in each quadrant) that at the same time will constitute the defensive system.

There are four positions with the point higher than the hand and four positions with the point lower than the hand. Of these eight positions, four are with the hand in supination, four with hand in pronation. It is the combination of hand and blade position which defines the positions in fencing.

The names of the positions are given sequentially in order of discovery and go from one to eight, in English. The terms used in international competition for the positions, in "Latinized French," are prime, second, tierce, quarte, quinte, sixte, septime, and octave.

HAND POSITIONS

The positions are defined for a right-handed fencer. For left-handed fencers, replace right by left.

The four positions with the point higher than the hand are:

Sixte   Hand in supination, to the right so as to protect against any attack coming to this side.

Tierce   Same position as sixte, except that the hand is in pronation.

Quarte   Hand in supination, on the left side of the target, protecting against any attack coming to this side.

Quinte   Same as quarte, except that the hand is in pronation.

The four positions with the point lower than the hand are:

Octave   Hand to the right, in supination.

Seconde   Same as octave, except that the hand is in pronation.

Septime   Hand is on the left side, in supination.

Prime   Presents some peculiarity in that, in view of turning the hand in supination while keeping it to the left, the forearm has to come to an almost horizontal position. Prime represents the first defensive move that comes naturally when one has to disengage the rapier from its scabbard at the beginning of a duel.

EN-GARDE POSITION

The classical definition of the en-garde is that it is the position that allows a fencer to be equally ready to attack or defend himself at any moment during a bout. The ability to move freely with balance and control is a determining factor in launching a successful attack or in successfully deflecting a thrusting action from the opponent.

En-garde position

Undoubtedly the possibility of scoring will be greatly increased with a surprise attack. This can be achieved if the action is not telegraphed by a shifting of the body, thus signaling the intention of the attacker. As fencers are constantly in motion, one can see how the en-garde position plays an important role in the effectiveness and success of a fencer.

Preparatory Position

Place the heels together with feet at a right angle. The front or leading foot, the right one for a right-handed fencer, points toward the opponent. The legs are straight, the body is erect, and the shoulders are relaxed. The rear arm rests along the body, fingers straight, while the arm holding the weapon points toward the floor at a spot a few feet ahead of the front foot. The trunk of the body is slightly turned to offer the minimum profile without muscle tension. The head faces the opponent.

To fall en-garde, place the front foot forward at a distance of about one and a half feet, front heel on a perpendicular line passing through the heel of the back foot. Bend equally on both knees in a sitting-like position so that the knees come to a position situated in the same plane going through the toes. Bend the right arm (or left arm if left-handed), the forearm relatively horizontal with hand palm up and the elbow about a hand's distance from the waist. At the same time, raise the back arm in an arched position, the elbow at shoulder level, the hand falling naturally from the wrist. Relaxation of the back hand is important, for it allows the fencer to check on his overall relaxation. When holding a weapon, the tip should be pointed toward the opponent's eyes.

Analysis

For the best possible balance in motion, the feet must be constantly flat on the floor and at a right angle to each other so as to allow the most flexible base from which the maximum speed and thrusting motion can be developed. The build of the individual plays an important role in determining how deeply to bend the knees. A low position is rarely required in fencing and is detrimental to quick and fluid movement, particularly in lunging. Too little bending limits the ability of the fencer to use his leg muscles and stiffens him. The fencer must learn through drills and trials what his best bending position is. Most likely it will be close to the general definition given above.

Ideally, the trunk should be straight to avoid any muscular tension. However, a tall fencer needs to lean slightly forward—*not by moving the shoulder down,* but by shifting the center of gravity slightly forward. (The center of gravity is situated a few inches below the navel.) A short fencer, on the other hand, can develop a more forceful attack when the weight of the body is slightly on the back leg. This concerns the relationship of leverage, mass, and speed.

For instruction purposes, the hand holding the weapon should be kept with the palm up. This position allows the greatest control of the point and freedom of blade motion, and consequently, greatest point accuracy. Holding the weapon with palm up also helps control the elbow position, which tends to move out of line, resulting in too much shoulder action.

Often coaches forget that arm extension should start from the elbow, not from the shoulder. The latter movement is frequently left uncorrected with beginners. Using the shoulder in extending the arm may make the action more forceful, but it tends to telegraph and supplies a momentum that makes control of the point and of the subsequent action very difficult.

The degree of arm extension in the en-garde position can vary somewhat. It depends on the tactical intent and the type of opponent. If the fencer relies on his defense, the arm bent closer to the waist facilitates the parry. A three-quarter extension of the arm favors the attack. The blade position also has to be adjusted for tactical purposes.

Some schools, such as the Italian, favor the greatest possible profiling of the trunk to offer the minimum target. In the process, the feet tend to take a crossing position, thus requiring more muscle efforts to maintain balance and position.

THE LUNGE

The French use the term "fente" to define the leg motion in the thrusting attack and "development" for the combination of the arm extension and leg motion. In other words, lunge should apply to leg action only. However, the extension of the sword arm precedes the lunge. The lunge by itself does not constitute an attack; it is only the vehicle of the attack. The name of the attack is derived solely from the blade motion—for example: disengage, one-two, and so on. In the lunge, the sword arm is extended prior to the leg action, which occurs a split second ahead (or in some cases at the same time) of the lunge.

To execute the lunge, the leading foot is projected forward with the heel almost gliding on the floor until the foot rests flat on the floor. The front knee is situated vertically above the middle of the foot. The foreleg and the thigh form a right angle, while the knee is kept from turning in.

Lunge

Complementing this motion, the back leg is rapidly and completely extended with a snappy action from the knee to add dynamic leverage to the lunge. At the same time the back arm is brought to a position parallel with the back leg, fingers stretched out. The back foot is kept firmly flat on the floor in the process to give maximum support to the leg action.

It is difficult to prove whether the action of the rear arm does or does not add speed to the lunge. However, the rear arm's action is essential in the recovery from the lunge and helps keep the balance at all times.

During the lunge, the position of the trunk should be controlled so that it does not participate in the lunging action by almost falling over the front leg. The trunk should be kept as erect as possible as it will affect the recovery process and subsequent fencing action.

The Recovery

The *backward* recovery results from a dual action of the legs and a quick motion of the rear arm. First, bend the rear knee while pushing backward from the heel of the front foot (lift the toes first). To help the latter come quickly into the original en-garde position, raise the left arm in a curling motion, as if pulling the body with the left hand firmly gripping a fixed object behind the fencer. The snappier the movement of the left arm and of the back knee, the quicker the recovery.

In the *forward* recovery, the same elements enter into consideration. The push is done with the back foot while the weight of the body is shifted slightly forward, the back foot brought under the body at the proper distance from the front foot with knees bent. The action is generally helped by the motion of the left arm coming sharply to its curled position. The fencer should be cautioned to execute the recovery strictly by the action of the legs rather than by the muscles of the back. This avoids an up and down movement detrimental to balance and protects against a possible back injury from the repetition of a twisting wrong movement.

FOOTWORK

The way a fencer moves on the strip generally reveals the level of his technique and effectiveness during a bout. However, mobility alone is not the formula for winning or becoming a good fencer!

The forward motion is called *advance* and the backward motion *retreat*. There are different ways to advance, but the classical and simplest way is the most efficient. To advance: Raise the toes of the front foot so that the heel can be moved forward, skimming over the floor a short distance (about a foot and a half), the rear foot following immediately for the same relative distance. At the end of the step, the fencer should be in the same en-garde position without having to readjust his body or leg position. The advance can be made also by moving the back foot first close to the front foot, keeping the knees bent. The front foot is then placed forward in the same manner as above.

The *jump* is a quick, short motion executed with both feet leaving the floor almost simultaneously. However, the feet should stay as close to the floor as possible during this motion.

Finally, the *passe avant* is a forward movement, which does not have much practical use, but is a good preparation for a form of attack called the fleche. To proceed, pass the back foot ahead of the front foot while executing a rolling motion on the sole of the front foot. The front foot is then quickly replaced in its forward position as soon as the rear foot has reached the floor. (The fleche is discussed in more detail in the chapter on sabre.)

To retreat, the reverse process of the advance is applied. The rear foot moves backward in a gliding motion, followed by the front foot covering about the same distance. The knees remain bent and the trunk of the body erect. In another way, the front foot moves first, passing behind the back foot. The back foot then moves backward to resume the en-garde position. This way of retreating is used especially when a fencer wishes to move part of the body target away from the opponent's attack.

The *jump backward* requires that the initial motion be made with the front foot while the rear foot moves backward. Both feet land on the floor practically at the same time.

The *passe arrière* is executed by moving the front foot backward while passing behind the rear foot. When the former reaches the floor, the other foot then moves backward an equal distance to resume the en-garde position.

Analysis

The ability to pursue an opponent without giving him an opportunity to develop his own attack or to withdraw out of reach in a split second is important in modern fencing competition. Constant movement forward and backward in order to keep the "right distance" requires conditioning and drilling. Its aim is to facilitate rapid balanced movement and agility on the strip.

Effective footwork depends greatly upon the fencer's en-garde position and avoidance of swinging back and forth or up and down while advancing or retreating. Any shift of body weight must be done by moving the center of gravity and *not* by leaning forward or backward with a shoulder or the upper part of the trunk. The steps should be as short as possible to avoid a "floating" movement during which the fencer is susceptible to attack by the opponent and in no position to deflect it.

Footwork should be smooth to avoid telegraphing any intention to the opponent. Smooth motion adds to the force and the surprise effect of the action.

The tendency in advance or retreat is to stretch either the front or the back leg instead of keeping the knees constantly bent so that the shoulders move constantly level parallel to the floor. The "up-and-down" motion not only delays one's actions but also reduces the ability to reach farther with the lunge, thus limiting the development of one's game.

The Advance-Lunge

This is a combination of a step forward followed immediately by a lunge. The step can be executed at different speeds and *tempos* according to the need and strategic necessity. Usually the advance-lunge is executed at a quick tempo to surprise the opponent and gain the right distance for developing the attack. However, it can start with a slow, gliding motion of the front foot followed by the back foot moving forward quickly. The lunge follows immediately.

Another way to do the advance-lunge is the *balestra,* used mostly by sabre fencers, although it can be used with all weapons. It is particularly useful for short fencers. The balestra is a small jump that starts by projecting the front foot forward. The back foot catches up quickly with the leading one so that both feet land on the floor at practically the same time. Upon landing, the front foot starts immediately for the lunge.

Flèche is a French expression meaning either "arrow" or "direction." It connotes speed. However, in fencing this action gains its effectiveness from its surprise rather than from greater speed, and allows the fencer to score from a farther distance than would a lunge.

The fleche is executed by extending the sword arm while moving the body's center of gravity sharply forward to accelerate the forward-springing action of the front leg. The back foot leaves the floor to land in front of the leading foot to regain balance. With this forward momentum, the fencer proceeds with quick, short strides after the attack is completed. The fleche can be executed from the en-garde position, from a half-lunging or lunging position, or after an advance.

Analysis

During the advance-lunge, whether slow or fast, keep the knees bent at all times to be in the best position to execute the decisive action at the appropriate moment and with maximum effectiveness. Picture a tiger preparing himself to jump over his prey: he invariably crouches deeply before the attack!

The tendency in the balestra is to execute the jump by rising too high above the floor. The result is that the momentum given to the lunge (which is the main purpose of the balestra) is somewhat reduced by landing too hard on the floor. When so executed, the action is susceptible to a successful counterattack. Consider the balestra as a means to carry a quick advance-lunge action rather than a long, powerful action.

In the fleche, the usual tendency is to stretch the front leg too soon with the loss of balance. This hinders a dynamic action that could come from leg extension and forces the front foot to leave the floor too soon. The result is reduction of speed and acceleration and in the maximum distance to be reached.

DISTANCE

Distance in fencing is based on the maximum reach a fencer can attain with the extension of the arm and a lunge. It is probably one of the most

Lunging distance for taller fencer

Lunging distance for shorter fencer

important factors in modern competition, particularly when two fencers are of different height or speed.

A tall fencer will try to keep the longest and safest distance to be able to use his reach with the maximum effectiveness. The short fencer, facing a much taller opponent, must seek a closer distance to be in a position to deliver his attack without being stopped by his opponent.

The ability to gain or break the distance requires excellent footwork and a precise evaluation of one's own distance of attack as well as that of the opponent. In all weapons three distances have to be considered:

1. Short distance, which is the distance of riposting.
2. Middle distance, or lunging distance.
3. Long distance, which is the distance of fleching.

Analysis

The three distances can be accurately defined because they occur in very definite situations. However, while bouting and until these situations present themselves, distance will vary. The primary object is to keep a safe distance from the opponent (at least until evaluation of his game has been completed) or to sustain the distance of attack until the opportunity is created or becomes available for an offensive action. The distance has to be evaluated with every opponent, but must become instinctive, adaptable, and accurate.

The ability to control the distance during a bout depends on the way the fencer moves and his footwork. The fencer who controls the distance usually controls the bout. Whoever controls the bout usually has the better chance of winning.

In the beginning, the fencer has to make a conscious effort to keep the right distance. This will probably reduce his concentration. Nevertheless, no effort should be spared in developing a sense of distance.

Given the above, one can see why the en-garde position is so important: It is the key to proper footwork. Whatever the mode of displacement, it has to be done smoothly to be able to gain distance without alerting the opponent. Jumping back and forth could be one way to fool the opponent about distance. However, if done repeatedly it may become an ingrained habit in the fencer and prove difficult to change later on. Such movement should be only part of a tactical system rather than the only strategy used by the fencer.

Specific exercises aimed at helping beginners to master distance are recommended. For example: While two fencers face each other, one fencer leads and the other tries to keep a constant distance as the partner moves back and forth using different steps at different tempos and speeds. This exercise requires concentration and is very helpful in giving fencers a sense of distance.

THE ENGAGEMENT

The engagement is the action of contacting the opponent's blade. It may be executed with more or less pressure on the blade depending on the purpose behind the action.

There are as many engagements as there are positions in fencing. For example: If the contact is made on the sixth line, it is called sixth engagement. The engagement consists of a displacement of one's blade, moving the point first so as to use the shortest distance between the two blades.

To get the maximum tactile sense and better control, contact should be made between the first and second thirds of the opponent's blade, while the hand holding the blade takes a position to cover the line of engagement.

The *change of engagement* and *double change of engagement:* Fencers who have already made blade contact may find it necessary to seek an engagement in a more favorable line (position). They change their engagement by moving the point under the opponent's blade and making contact on the opposite side in a circling motion. A double change of engagement

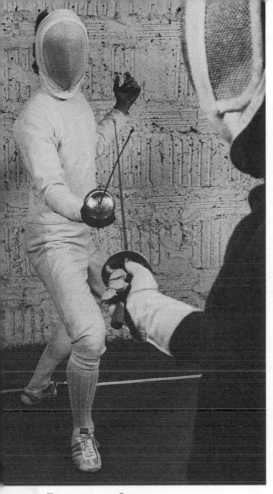

Engagement of **quarte**   Engagement of sixte

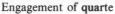consists of executing two successive changes, one on each side, without moving the hand from the initial position.

During all these motions, point control through finger action is extremely important. Speedy execution will influence the success of consecutive attacks and a possible defensive move that might be necessary if the opponent decides to develop his own offensive action.

Analysis

Engagements and changes of engagement are an excellent exercise for developing fingering, point control, speed, and hand firmness. Despite the trend in modern fencing to avoid blade play until the moment of attack, both engagements and changes of engagement are also extremely important in a tactical sense. They facilitate control on the opponent's blade and, subsequently, of the game.

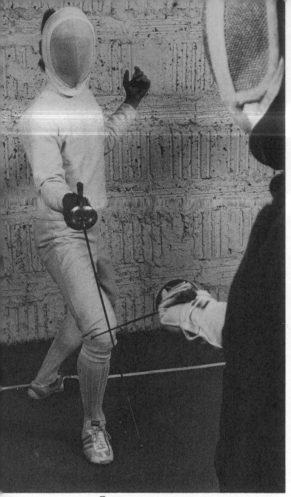

Octave engagement   Septime engagement

They can be used to block an opponent's offensive action or to provoke his attack under conditions unfavorable to him so that counterattack or defensive moves can be successfully achieved. They are a useful means for preparing an action or delaying the opponent's reaction.

Engagements or changes of engagement should not be executed without a reason. They are a safe way of gaining the right distance before developing an attack.

SIMPLE ATTACKS

An attack is an offensive action that can be executed either with a lunge or a fleche. It can be simple or compound.

The *simple attack* is an offensive action executed in one tempo with one point movement. There are three simple attacks. The first, which takes its name from the direction of its execution, is the **straight thrust** (coup droit). It is a combination of the arm extension and the lunge with the point moving in a straight line. It is usually executed when the line of engagement, either high or low, is left open by the opponent. In the high line, the hand is in supination. In the low line, the hand should be turned in pronation with the point higher than the hand.

Analysis

Although easy to execute, the straight thrust, to be successful, requires distance, timing, and speed. It will surprise if the attack is not telegraphed, enabling the opponent to parry in time. It will also be successful when the circumstances are favorable:

1. When the opponent is unprepared (relaxes his defense).
2. When the opponent is recovering from a lunge.
3. When the opponent makes mechanical motions with no tactical intent, such as feints or changes of engagement.

The **disengagement** gets its name from the action of getting away from blade contact. Let us suppose that the blades of the fencers are in contact.

Disengagement and lunge

Disengage in quarte

To execute a disengagement, move the point beneath the opponent's blade, the point describing a half-circle with finger action while the arm is extended. The lunge follows immediately.

The disengagement can be executed from a high line to a high line, for example: from sixte to quarte. In this case, it is recommended that the hand be kept in supination. It also can be used effectively from high line to low line. In this case, the point does not describe a horizontal half-circle but a vertical semicircular motion. In the process, the hand moves from a supinated to a pronated position. The hand at the end of the movement will be lower than the shoulder and the point higher than the hand, forming an angle at the wrist. In the disengage executed from the low line to low line position, the point is moved *over* the opponent's blade.

Analysis

To achieve a successful disengagement the point motion should be as slight as possible and the point should move forward progressively in a stretched corkscrew or helicoidal fashion. The thumb and index action in the disengagement contributes to the speed with which the attack is delivered. A too-wide motion with the arm slows down the execution and enables the opponent to parry successfully. Swiftness and development of arm and lunging action in one tempo are necessary elements.

Straight thrust and lunge

Tactically, the conditions for executing a successful disengage are the same as with the straight thrust. However, some actions against the opponent's blade, such as a "beat" or a "pressure," before the disengagement will increase the chances of scoring.

The **cutover** (coupe) is a form of disengagement that allows scoring in a different line from the line of engagement. As its name indicates, its executions take the form of a cutting motion. The blade is passed over the opponent's point with a combination of finger, wrist, and forearm motion, followed by a rapid extension on the other side of the opponent's blade with the lunge immediately following.

Beat: disengage and lunge

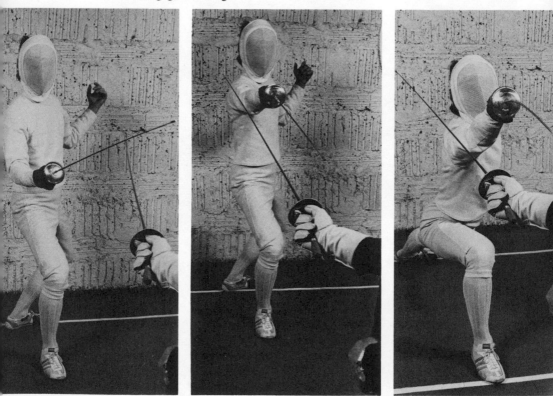

Coupe

The cutover is executed almost exclusively in the high line and is very difficult to parry, although the ample motion used makes it easy to anticipate. The cutover from a low line (octave or seconde) is sometimes useful in riposting. It is executed by withdrawing the elbow backward, while the blade is moved over the opponent's point.

Analysis

To execute the coupe do not use only the fingers or wrist. This makes the blade move into almost a vertical position in order to pass over the opponent's point, thus delaying the end (finale) of the attack and giving the opponent an opportunity to counterattack or withdraw to a safe distance.

A slight, quick action of the forearm eliminates the need for a vertical position of the blade.

On the other hand, a well-executed cutover can be done with a lateral as well as a circular parry, for the blade does not come in horizontally as in other attacks, but in an angular way, making it difficult for the opponent to choose the right moment to parry.

The best defense against the cutover is a transverse parry—high septime.

To avoid a possible counterattack, the cutover should be preceded by some preparation as an attack on the blade such as a beat or a pressure.

The technique of execution in the simple attacks is an important factor that allows a fencer to use his maximum speed whenever necessary. However, to deliver these actions successfully, the fencer also must have a sense of "à propos" and acceleration. "À propos" concerns timing, and acceleration concerns control of the speed with which the attack should be delivered.

Simple attacks require a correct evaluation of the defensive reflexes of the opponent and, subsequently, his ability to execute them at different tempos. Simple attacks can be executed when an engagement has been completed, when the opponent is in the process of engaging, or when preceded by an engagement. This sequence in executing the attack is particularly useful for teaching.

Fencing Phrase

A fencing *phrase* is an exchange of fencing actions between two fencers that leads eventually to a hit. The classic phrase includes: an attack on the part of one of the fencers, then a parry and riposte from the opponent. The phrase may be continued if necessary or may involve a more complex exchange between the two fencers.

Right-of-Way

Right-of-way is the privilege accorded to a fencer who, through his threatening action, forces his opponent into the defensive. A threatening action is characterized by the arm being extended with the point of the weapon aimed at the target.

PARRIES

The *parry* is a defensive move intended to deflect the opponent's blade in

1st parry (prime)   2nd parry (seconde)   3rd parry (tierce)

its attempt to reach the target. The parry takes its name from the position
of the hand in which the defensive move will end. For instance, the parry
of quarte means that the attack has been deflected with a blade motion
ending in quarte position. So it is for the name of any other parry: sixte,
septime, and so on. The parries can be classified as follows:

Lateral The defensive blade motion goes from right to left (or vice
versa) while staying in either the high or low lines. The control of the point
and the position of the hand in executing the parry are determining factors
in the completion of a successful riposte. From sixte position to parry
quarte: The point moves slightly ahead to meet the oncoming attack while
the hand takes its position in quarte to cover the target. Use the edge of the

4th parry (quarte)   5th parry (quinte)   6th parry (sixte)

blade to make contact. Avoid unnecessary turning of the hand or the wrist, for it tends to displace the point far out of line. To parry sixte from quarte: Use the reverse process.

Lateral parries in the low line also require that the point be moved ahead of the hand and slightly out of line to afford complete protection against an angular attack.

7th parry (septime)

Circular (or counter) The point describes a circular motion in the defensive move, picking up the opponent's blade and bringing it outside the target line in the process. To execute counter sixte: Beginning with the hand in sixte position, drop the point, by means of finger motion, below the oncoming attacking blade. Then, using the momentum generated, continue the circling motion to bring the opponent's blade back into the starting sixte line. The action is executed clockwise, with the opponent's blade coming

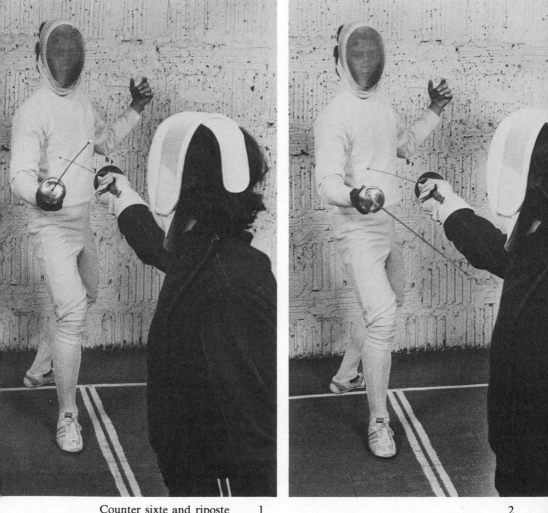

Counter sixte and riposte   1   2

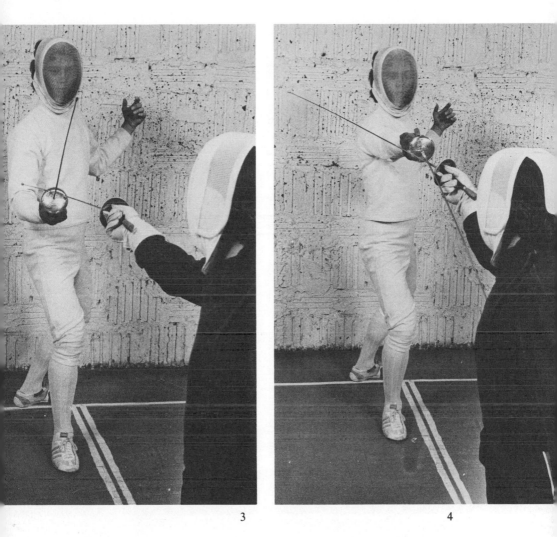

3   4

in the inside line. To execute counter quarte: From the quarte position, the point executes a counterclockwise movement to pick up the blade coming in the inside line.

When making counter parries, avoid using too much wrist action, for it tends to cause wide motion of the point without increasing the efficiency of the parry. The contraction of the last three fingers during the final point motion of the parry should be sufficiently forceful to resist any strong attempt by the opponent to overcome the blade.

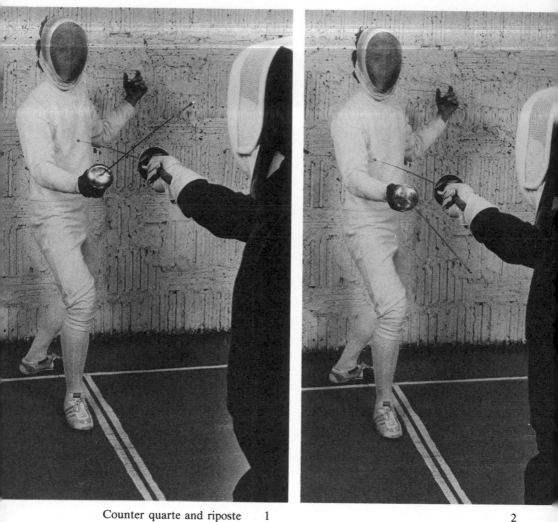

Counter quarte and riposte   1   2

The circular parries executed in the low line are executed with the point passing *over* the opponent's blade and with the same finger action.

Semicircular   The blade executes a semicircle with the point going from a high line to a low line (or vice versa). In either case, the point goes through the inside line to pick up the opponent's blade and to bring it either into a high or a low line. Examples: from sixte to octave (or seconde) and vice versa; from quarte to septime, and vice versa. If the semicircular parry finishes in the low line, the point should move slightly out of line and the forearm should lower slightly to assure complete covering of the target.

The displacement of blade and hand in deflecting the attacking blade allow any of the above parries to be accomplished in two different ways:

1. With a sharp beat (done with finger action accompanied by a slight wrist action) on the middle of the opponent's blade.

2. With the opponent's attack being deflected with a firm hand in a blocking motion rather than by a hitting on the blade.

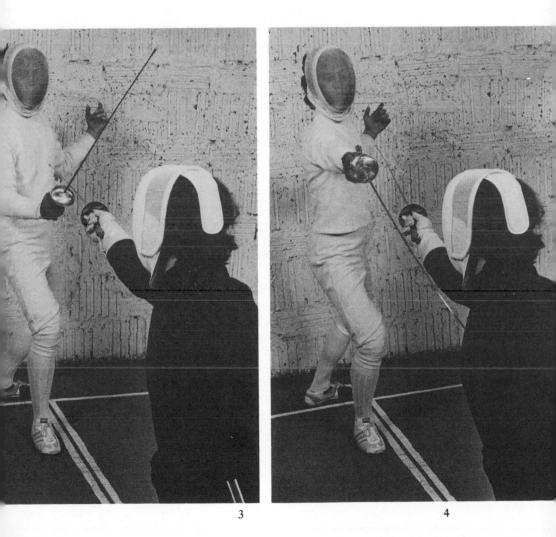

3   4

Analysis

The parry can be executed either at the beginning of the opponent's attack or when the attack has been completely developed. Both have their advantages and weaknesses. When to execute the parry depends on the tactical intent and the decision as to which would be more successful. In both cases the parry must deflect the point of the attacking blade sufficiently so as to allow the right-of-way for the riposte (return attack).

As much as possible, the parry should be made with the strong part of the blade to get the maximum control over the weak part of the attacking blade without unnecessary tension or tightening of the hand.

The manner in which the parry is made will influence the speed of the start and the execution of the riposte. Too much force or unnecessary muscular tension delays reflex and reduces speed. Pay special attention to moving the blade and hand at the same time and keeping them in the same plane so that the threatened target will be well protected.

The *lateral* parry is the most natural and easiest to execute. However, to be most effective it requires constant training to control the point and hand position.

The *circular* parry, in which the attacking blade moves from inside to outside the target, should be executed mainly with the fingers to avoid a too-wide motion with the point.

The *semicircular* and the *diagonal* parries have some advantages against some specific attacks. However, they are easy to foil.

The quarte parry is probably the one most commonly used in competition, for it covers the main part of the target. Octave (or seconde, depending on whether the hand is in pronation or supination) protects against attack on the flank in the low line.

Septime, which is a diagonal action, can sweep a lot of attacks directed toward the inside line.

Finally, high septime, which is extremely effective against cutover (coupe) attacks, raises the point from a septime position to an almost horizontal position of the blade, the hand following the point motion and rising above shoulder level.

These parries can stop practically any attacks coming from any direction and should serve as a basis for developing a complete defensive game. They should sometimes be combined with the retreat for added security or with an advance to break into the opponent's attack. The latter move, however, is risky, for it requires correct judgment of the kind of attack to be expected and of the right moment to parry with the advance.

RIPOSTE AND COUNTER RIPOSTE

The riposte is an offensive action following the successful parry of an attack.

The counter riposte is also an offensive action following a successful parry, but it follows the successful parry of a riposte (or counter riposte).

Technique that applies to the riposte consequently applies to the counter riposte as well. What distinguishes these two actions is the sequence in which they are made. In terms of sequence, what differentiates the attack from the riposte is that the riposte is executed by the defender. Subsequently, the first counter riposte is executed by the attacker.

As with the attack, the riposte is either simple—if executed with one point motion—or compound if two or more point motions are involved. The riposte can be executed immediately (tac-au-tac) or with a delayed tempo (à temps perdu).

The simple riposte is either a direct or indirect riposte. The riposte is "direct" when executed in the same line in which the parry has taken place: solely by a straight thrust. The riposte is indirect when it ends in a line

Sixte parry and direct riposte

Sixte parry and riposte to low line

different from the one in which the parry has taken place: disengage, or cutover.

The execution of these ripostes follows the same principles as the simple attacks. They can be delivered from the en-garde position, with an advance, a lunge, an advance lunge, or a fleche. The speed of the opponent's recovery and the tactical intent are the determining factors in riposting from the en-garde position, with an advance, or with a lunge, etc.

Analysis

Some ripostes are a purely reflex action in which speed is the dominant factor. Other ripostes—particularly the compound ones and those executed

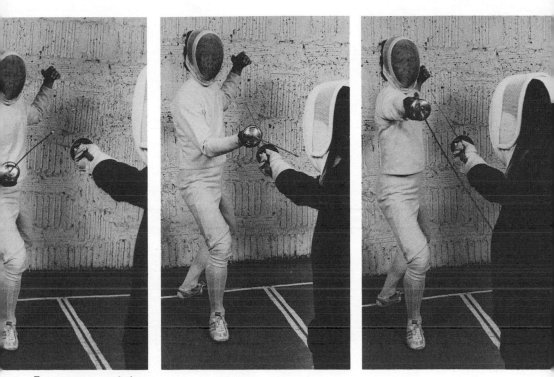

Parry quarte and riposte

with a delayed tempo—require judgment and tactical decision based on observation of the opponent's reactions.

Basically the direct riposte follows a parry made with a beat, while the indirect riposte follows a parry made with either a beat or an opposition. The choice of parry to be used is based on the opponent's reaction, which varies from fencer to fencer.

On the other hand, the decision as to which kind of riposte to use always depends on the way the opponent reacts when his attack has been parried and on his ability to use the appropriate riposte. Thus it is important for the fencer to notice immediately his opponent's reactions.

In most instances the riposte made immediately following the parry requires only an arm motion to reach the target. However, if the opponent has recovered rapidly before the riposte can be made, or if an extra step backward has been taken at the time of the parry as a matter of safety, it may be necessary to use an advance or a lunge (or fleche) to reach with the riposte.

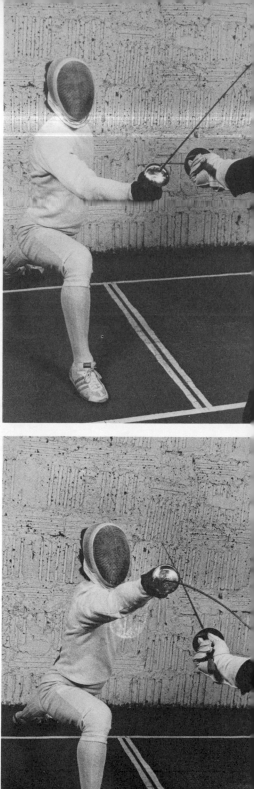

Counter riposte

If the speed of the opponent's reaction after his unsuccessful attack prevents the use of a simple riposte, a compound riposte is most likely required, such as a one-two. In this case, a quick point-motion feint, without even extending the arm, may be used to block the opponent's parry immediately and score ahead of his next move.

The compound riposte is not recommended against a fencer who systematically remises after his unsuccessful attack. The riposte with a taking-of-the-blade, "croisé" particularly, or bind, will solve this problem.

The fencer should learn to deliver the riposte to the different parts of the target to be in a position to select the appropriate one against the different type of fencers he will meet in a competition. Constant drilling to develop point accuracy is necessary and will increase the chances of scoring.

Special attention should be given to arm action during the riposte. Too often the riposte is made with a locked arm, so that fencers, to reach the target without overshooting, have to retreat at the time of the riposte. In many instances the riposte is short or the retreat allows the opponent the opportunity to parry the riposte or to recover out of reach.

Ripostes at close distance are often neglected during drilling sessions. In competitions most attacks, whether successful or not, bring the fencers to a close distance. This means that the riposte must be executed primarily with the point moving toward the opponent and with minimum arm extension to reach the target. In most instances the riposte should be done with the arm extending only about halfway.

COMPOUND ATTACKS

A compound attack is an offensive action that includes one or more feints before the final hit. A feint is a simulation of an attack. It usually is made with the sword arm fully extended.

The feint is used primarily to make the opponent react, usually with a defensive move, and then to act upon his reaction (by deceiving his parry) while executing a final action with a lunge.

Feints can be slow or fast, long or short, depending on the opponent's reactions. The feint can be simple or compound. A simple feint corresponds to the classifications of the simple attack: *straight feint* or *disengage feint* or *cutover feint.* A compound feint is a combination of two or more feints. For instance: a *one-two feint,* a *straight feint* and *disengage feint.*

The variety of feints has practically no limit. However, the use of too many feints tends to destroy their very purpose by giving the opponent time to recover from the effect of surprise, and allowing him to counterattack, or to get out of reach with a quick retreat.

There are as many compound attacks as there are combinations of two or more simple attacks. They can be preceded with an attack on the blade or a taking-of-the-blade. They can be executed with a lunge, an advance lunge, or an advance flèche.

The advance in the compound attack has several purposes: to gain distance, to surprise, and to reinforce or accentuate the effect of the feint. The advance can be made at a fast or slow pace, or with a break of tempo. In any event, coordination between point motion and leg action is essential to carry on a successful attack.

One-two from sixte engagement   1   2

Basic Compound Attacks

One-two. This compound attack begins with a disengage feint to provoke a *lateral parry*. The parry is then deceived by executing a second (reverse) disengage followed by an immediate lunge. Put more simply, the one-two is a compound attack made up of two consecutive disengages, the last one leading to a hit with a lunging motion.

Double. Like the one-two, it involves a disengage feint to provoke a *circular parry* and the deception of the parry while the lunge is executed. In the double compound attack the direction of the point is not reversed after the disengage feint, as in the one-two, but continues in a corkscrew-like motion to deceive the circular parry.

3   4

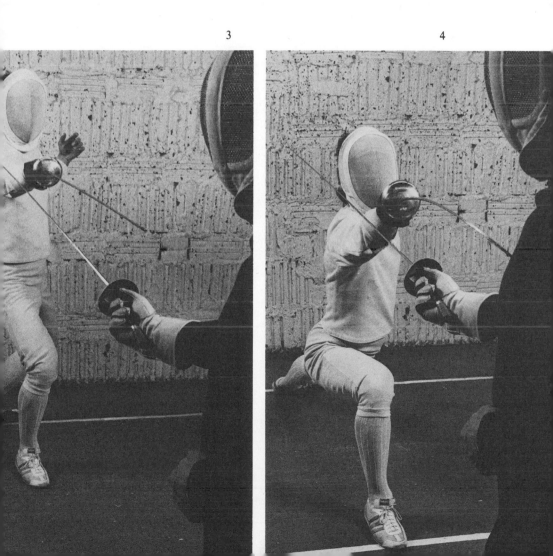

Straight Feint–Disengage.   When fencers keep a long distance between themselves, the blades do not engage until the moment of the attack. It is then necessary to proceed with a straight feint to provoke the opponent into a defensive move. If the opponent reacts with a lateral parry, the defensive move will be deceived by a disengage. If after a straight feint the opponent reacts with, for example, a counter sixte, the deception will be done with a counter disengage and the compound attack is then called a *straight feint-deceive the counter sixte.*

Feint: low-high-low   1

2

3

4

Compound Attack Using Cutover.   The cutover as a feint can be made at middle distance, but it should not be overly used as it may draw a counterattack from the opponent when the point is withdrawn to pass over the opponent's blade. The cutover is much more effective as a final action in a compound attack as it does not require the evaluation of the opponent's parry. The cutover can deceive any lateral parry and also can go through a counter parry. When a cutover is used in a compound attack,

1

2 3

Feint: low-high

4

it takes the name of the feint plus that of the cutover or vice versa. For instance: straight feint–cutover, or cutover-disengage.

Analysis

For teaching purposes, the feint should precede the lunge so as to give the pupil time to concentrate on the extension of the arm and learn the manner in which to execute the feint, as well to prepare himself to deceive the coming parry.

The coach should caution the student not to "throw" the point with the arm and not to lean forward exaggeratedly. It is important that after the feint the en-garde position be such that the legs are ready to spring quickly for the final action. Later, the fencer learns to coordinate the lunging motion with the feint to gain penetration and momentum while executing the complete attack.

Keep in mind that the lunge in a compound attack starts during or at the end of the action preceding the final move. The tempo used for the attack or the mode of attack to be used—for example: with an advance or a jump —will determine at which point the lunge should be developed in relation to the feint.

The position of the point in the feint has some bearing in inducing the opponent to make a definite parry. For instance, the point placed at the opponent's hand level, but not too close, will likely provoke him to use a lateral parry. The point aimed above and close to the hand may bring a circular parry. The point aimed below the hand might induce a predictable semicircular parry.

The choice of an attack is primarily determined by the kind of reaction the fencer expects from his opponent. On the other hand, the type of feint used in the compound attacks determines how the opponent will react. Thus the manner in which the feint is carried out is crucial for a successful hit.

Defense Against Compound Attacks

When the opponent's attack is simple, a single parry is usually sufficient to deflect the blade. When the opponent is using feints and compound attacks, more than one parry may be required.

The best defensive system against compound attacks is to ignore and not react to the different feints or preparations and to make the parry at the end of the opponent's attack with a single appropriate blade motion. This requires that the fencer keep one line entirely closed to attacks, thus forcing the opponent to make his attack on a predetermined target. However, the constant use of this defensive system exposes the fencer to certain tactical actions by his opponent that eventually succeed in penetrating his defense.

Combination of Parries

The answer against the compound attack is a combination of parries and should be part of every fencer's defensive system. Its aim is threefold: to lead the opponent into executing a specific attack, to prepare for the final parry, and to change the pattern and tempo of the defensive moves. It may also lead the opponent to make his final move into a line that will be closed or easily protected.

The first parry of the combination should be made smoothly, with point control, so that the following parry can be executed with maximum speed and firmness. The final parry should not be made too soon, to avoid being deceived. It should also be of a different kind whenever possible.

Parries should be combined with footwork while keeping correct distance at the same time. Retreats should be made so that the target can be reached either with an extension of the arm or a lunge.

Here are some examples of combination of parries:

Sixte; counter-sixte
Quarte; counter-quarte
Seconde; sixte
Octave; quarte
Counter-sixte; septime
Seconde; sixte; counter-sixte
Octave; quarte; counter-quarte

PREPARATION OF ATTACKS

Preparation in fencing is defined as action or movement that a fencer uses before developing his attack. This general definition includes such actions as a feint, an engagement, an advance, and so on. However, for our purposes, preparations of attacks have been divided into two categories, each one having its own basic purpose and characteristics. All of these preparations involve blade action against the opponent's blade. What differentiates them is the way in which the blade action is made: whether *it controls* the opponent's blade until completion of the attack, *or not.*

Attacks on the Blade

There are three attacks on the blade:
1. the beat
2. the pressure
3. the expulsion

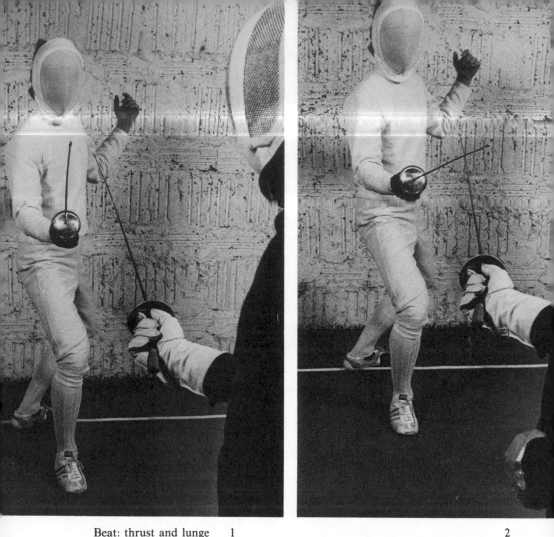

Beat: thrust and lunge   1   2

The *beat* is a "tap," a striking action executed with the upper medium part of the blade against the same relative portion of the opponent's blade, with more or less intensity or sharpness depending on the reaction desired from the opponent. It should be executed with finger action or the arm rather than with the wrist only to avoid any possible deception on the part of the opponent.

The beat as a preparation for an attack serves different purposes. A strong beat may open the line in which one wishes to develop an attack: *beat straight,* for instance. On the other hand, a strong beat may bring a strong reaction—or no reaction at all—depending on the fencer. A light beat is more subtle and serves a better purpose at times in that it does not alert the opponent's defensive reflexes, thus allowing the succeeding attack to pro-

3   4

gress with a *tempo* ahead. Fencers react differently to a beat depending on their natural reflex or their control of reflex reaction, their strength, and eventually their tactical intention.

Generally, the purpose of the beat is to provoke a delay in the opponent's reaction for a split second, thus allowing more time for execution of the succeeding attack (simple or compound). The beat is particularly efficient against a fencer who keeps his arm fully extended. In this case, it must be said that the beat is also necessary before developing the attack in order to get the right-of-way.

One should note the following about the right-of-way in relation to the beat. A beat on the opponent's blade does not constitute the right-of-way. It *allows* the use of the right-of-way on the condition that the attack follows the beat immediately. Any delay between the beat and the consecutive attack allows the opponent to take advantage of the situation if he wishes and to develop his own offensive action.

The *pressure* is a springlike action (pressure and immediate release) on the opponent's blade. Its force depends on how firmly the opponent is holding his foil. It is executed with the upper medium part of the blade against the same part of the opponent's blade and requires a simple contraction of the fingers combined with a slight wrist action.

In the pressure, the blade contact is very short, just enough to provoke an immediate reaction from the opponent and to take advantage of it to execute the appropriate attack (either simple or compound). In some instances the pressure, like the beat, can be used to provoke the opponent's attack. Such use means that one must be prepared to use the appropriate defensive move. The general considerations discussed here concerning the beat apply equally to the pressure.

The *expulsion* is a combination of beat and pressure executed over the entire length of the opponent's blade, usually in a horizontal position. It is a whipping motion with the strong part of the blade against the weak part of the opponent's blade, followed by a brusque whipping motion forward along the opponent's blade. If he is unprepared, the opponent may be disarmed by this action. Tactically, however, the expulsion accomplishes little more than possibly a disarmament.

Attacks with Taking-of-the-Blade

While the attack on the blade is intended as a quick, crisp action, the attack with taking-of-the blade aims at controlling the opponent's blade until the completion of the action. There are four such attacks and all require the same two conditions: first, that the opponent's blade be in an almost horizontal position; second, that the opponent's arm be extended or almost completely extended. These two conditions are most likely to be fulfilled when the opponent is threatening the target or is bringing his attack to completion:

The Opposition   This can be defined as a straight thrust executed along the opponent's blade while exerting pressure on it (for instance: the sixte opposition). It is executed by contacting the opponent's blade on its weak part while extending the arm and exercising a constant pressure domination proportionate to the opponent's resistance. The point progresses forward until reaching the target.

Opposition

The Bind This takes the opponent's blade from a high line (without releasing contact at any time) and brings it into the opposite diagonal low line. Conversely, it can be executed from a low line to a high line (for instance: bind from sixte to septime, from quarte to octave or seconde, from septime to sixte, and so on).

Bind: quarte to octave   1   2

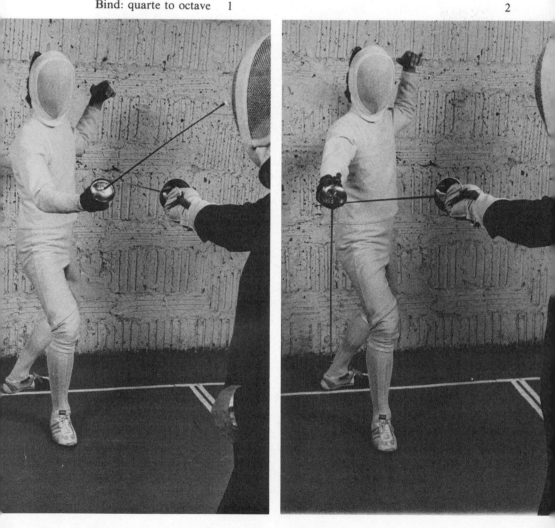

The Envelopment Some fencers call this a double binding, but this is not an accurate definition, for the opponent's blade is never carried to a different line during the envelopment. The envelopment takes the opponent's blade in one line and controls it while remaining in the same line through a wide circular motion of the blade. Blade contact is never released while the point progresses forward toward the target (for instance: envelopment of sixte, of seconde, and so on).

Envelopment

Envelopment: septime to sixte

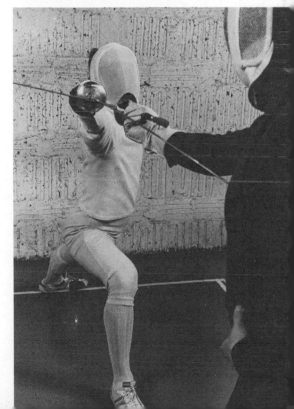

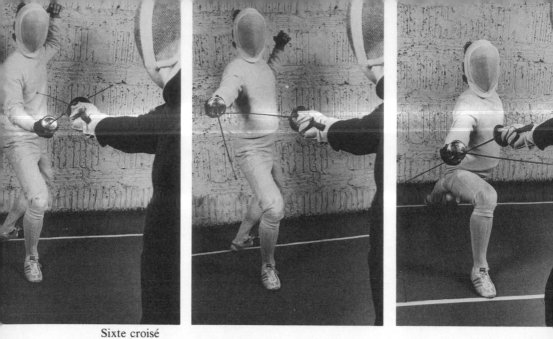

Sixte croisé

The Croisé The croisé may be defined as a semibind. It is executed by taking the opponent's blade in one line and bringing it into the opposite, but on the same side, low line (for instance: from quarte to septime, from sixte to octave, and so on).

Quarte croisé

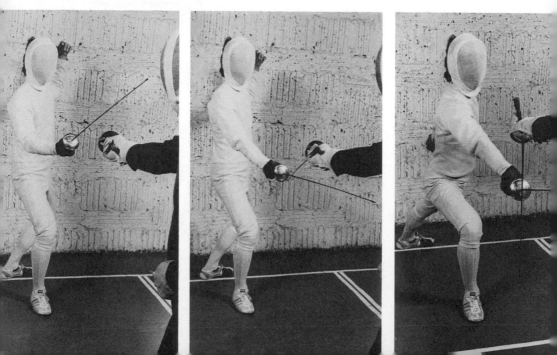

Analysis

As mentioned at the beginning of this chapter, a horizontal blade position is required for attacks with taking-of-the-blade. Execution of these attacks also requires identical technical conditions:

1. The taking of the opponent's blade should begin at its weak part.

2. Contact with the opponent's blade should be made with the strong part of the blade as close as possible to the guard. The ideal taking-of-the-blade

Septime parry and riposte

is to have the opponent's blade in contact with one's own strong part of the blade *and* guard, the combination forming a "pincer" that helps to maintain pressure and control of the opponent's blade.

3. The attacks should be executed with the point moving progressively toward the target.

4. The pressure to be exerted depends on the opponent's resistance in trying to close the threatened line.

5. Complete domination of the opponent's blade is necessary if the point is to be placed on the target.

All attacks with taking-of-the-blade can be executed in every line. All can be executed from the en-garde position and consequently can be considered as part of a defensive/offensive system. However, some of them are more practical when executed in one line than another. For instance, attacks with taking-of-the-blade ending in quarte (or septime) position require more lateral opposition to give complete cover during the action. This is particularly important in epee.

The quarte croisé and sixte croisé are extremely efficient actions, the former against right-handed fencers and the latter against left-handed fencers. (For a left-handed fencer, it is the reverse.)

The bind and the opposition offer protection against possible remise on the part of the opponent.

Although the attacks with taking-of-the-blade in foil may not offer as much practical use as the attack on the blade, practicing them is an excellent exercise for developing good control of the blade and hand position. Executed with the lunge, the attack with taking-of-the-blade has to be developed with the final blade motion, which may be a straight thrust or any other attack depending on the opponent's reaction and tactical purpose. In any event, the blade contact should not be ended too soon to avoid a possible counterattack.

If possible, the taking-of-the-blade should start with the hand in supination, even if the final attack ends with the hand in pronation.

COUNTERATTACKS

These are offensive or defensive-offensive actions executed against the opponent's attack. Although they can take different forms, they are generally classified into three categories: the *stop thrust, time thrust,* and *dérobement.*

The Stop Thrust   This is an offensive action that consists of "stopping" the opponent's attack with a simple offensive move (straight thrust or

Stop thrust against bent arm attack

disengage). To be valid the stop thrust must hit before the opponent's final action. Usually the stop thrust is executed at the very beginning of the opponent's attack. It surprises and tends to block the opponent's reflex, preventing him from completing the attack or delaying the final movement of his action. It is generally executed in a high or low line and usually accompanied by a half-lunge.

The determining factors in using counterattack are the opponent's tendency to start his attack with either a bent arm, wide blade motions accompanied with automatic advances or jumps, or too many feints in his search for an opening. The stop thrust requires excellent judgment combined with precise timing. Because of the risk involved in possibly misjudging the opponent's intention, it should be used sparingly. The best moment to execute the stop thrust is when the opponent moves the leading foot when beginning an advance or a jump, or at his very first feint. The risk in doing a stop thrust becomes greater as the opponent's attack is developed further.

The Time Thrust This is a defensive-offensive action that scores a hit while keeping the opponent's attack from arriving on the target. It can be compared to a parry and a riposte executed in the same tempo while intercepting the opponent's final motion. To some extent it is safer than the

Stop thrust against fleche

Time thrust

stop thrust. However, besides judgment and timing, it requires a perfect evaluation of the opponent's intention.

Some fencers have developed a fencing style based on the concept that all attacks can be intercepted with the help of the two time thrusts: the sixte, which blocks the line against any attack finishing in the outside line; and the seconde (or octave), which intercepts attacks ending in the inside line. However, to overcome this rather limited game requires only low and high feints executed judiciously. The time thrust can be very effective when used sparingly as part of a rounded tactical game.

To increase the effectiveness of the time thrust, the counterattack should be reinforced by a small lunging action, and before executing it the fencer should not telegraph his intention to counterattack. When the opponent's attack is expected to end in the sixte line, the time thrust (sixte opposition) is executed when the opponent's point is in the process of reaching the sixte line and must allow for the speed and tempo with which he delivers his attack. If the time thrust is executed too soon, the opponent can drop his point (voluntarily or not) and score in the low line. If it is executed too late, the opponent scores as his point reaches the target.

The time thrust in seconde is made as the first feint is being completed —for instance, in a one-two ending in the inside line—to block the path of the second disengage. Both time thrusts described above are executed with the arm moving forward while taking the sixte or seconde position, with the point directed toward the target and in the appropriate line.

The Dérobement (evasion)   This is the action of evading the opponent's *offensive* move. Usually the arm must be fully extended to induce the opponent to take the blade that is presented, then to avoid his attack on the blade or taking-of-the-blade with a disengage or a cutover in either a low or high line. The tactic is based on the principle of right-of-way, which is that a fencer must not attack against an extended arm unless he first deflects the opponent's threatening point. A fencer with a long arm and, consequently, with a long reach has a distinct advantage when using the dérobement.

VARIETY OF ATTACKS

The attacks included in this category have the same specific purpose: to be used against an opponent who parries successfully but does not riposte immediately or does not riposte at all. To take advantage of this situation, the fencer should either launch another attack or carry the same attack with a continuation in the same line.

The first instance is called a *redoublement* when preceded with a recovery forward (in some instances backward). An example is a one-two attack: immediate recovery followed immediately by a cutover attack executed with another lunge or a fleche.

If the second attack is executed while the fencer remains in the lunging position it is called *reprise*. For example: a beat disengage attack followed by a cutover at the end of the attack and while in the lunging position.

If the consecutive attack is made by simply replacing the point in the same line of the opponent's parry, while remaining in the lunge position, it is called *remise.*

The variety of attacks are an important part of a fencer's repertoire. They are extremely useful against fencers who are not riposting immediately (reprise) or tend to retreat and keep a long distance (redoublement), or to take advantage of any moment of hesitation on the part of the opponent after his defensive moves (remise).

The best defense against fencers using a variety of attacks is usually to change the distance at the time of the attack; to make the parry while advancing instead of retreating as expected; to riposte immediately or by using a riposte with a taking-of-the-blade, such as bind or croisé.

False Attack and Second Intention

Although a feint is a simulation of an attack, it usually implies the beginning of a compound attack and requires only the extension of the arm (combined or not with an advance or a retreat).

The *false attack* is an attack that is intended to fall short of the target. It is a simple or compound action, including the arm extension and a lunge, incompletely developed, but with enough penetration and depth to lure the opponent into reacting. The false attack also serves to probe the opponent's reactions.

The main purpose of the false attack, however, is *second intention,* which is any action or preparation on the part of a fencer to induce his opponent to execute an offensive or defensive motion, then to act upon his reaction to make the scoring hit. It can be a simple change of engagement, a feint to provoke a counterattack, or a false attack to induce him to parry and riposte. Second intention can be either defensive or offensive.

Second intention is *defensive* when the intent is to make the opponent attack under specific conditions so as to know the exact moment of his attack and the line in which to expect it. His attack will then be parried and riposted under the best possible conditions. Preparations with engagement or change of engagement (accompanied or not by an advance or retreat) to induce the opponent to attack are most useful.

It is *offensive* when the intent is to make the opponent react in a specific manner and to develop an attack that takes into consideration either his defensive move (parry) or counterattack. For instance: Make a false attack with a straight feint to force the opponent to react in quarte and immediately follow the false attack with a one-two while the lunge is brought to completion. Another example: Provoke a counterattack through either beat or attack feints and take over the opponent's blade with a taking-of-the-blade. This is then called counter time and is described in more detail in the following section.

In second intention distance is extremely important. If the preparation is made too close to induce the opponent to react, his attack may score before the parry can be completed. If it is too far away, the opponent can refuse to fall into the trap or, if he does, the distance still will not permit a successful riposte to reach the target.

The engagements or changes of engagement will trigger the opponent's offensive reflex if they do not reveal the second-intention tactic behind their execution. Therefore, perfect distance and the right preparation are the basic ingredients for a successful second-intention attack.

COUNTER TIME

Counter time is an offensive action executed after parrying a counterattack. For example: when a fencer advances with a long feint to induce the opponent to counterattack. At the beginning of the opponent's counterattack, he should immediately overtake the opponent's blade with a sixte opposition, which will be carried out with a lunge or a fleche to the target. Or, the fencer executes a one-two feint with a balestra. The opponent's counterattack being expected at the very moment the preparation is made, one should immediately overtake the opponent's blade with a bind, quarte to octave, which is carried out with a lunge or a fleche to the target.

Particularly effective against fencers whose game is based on counter-offensive actions, counter time requires anticipation of the opponent's action and of the exact moment of execution. The preparation for executing the counter-time action is directed toward inducing the opponent to counterattack in a specific line and then to parry-riposte his action. Preparations may consist of feints, advances, beat on the blade, and so on. A particularly important factor in provoking the expected reaction from the opponent is the tempo used by the fencer performing the counter-time action. The proper tempo seems either to eliminate in the opponent all notions of a possible trap or to make the preparation so real that the counterattack is almost instinctive. It is not so much the technique involved in the preparation as the tempo and meaning with which they are executed that are the determining factors.

Contrasts in tempo—slow to sharp and vice versa—should be used in the preparation. One or the other will trigger the reaction, depending on the opponent's condition.

Using the same tempo makes the opponent cautious and wary. He usually will not react unless a deeper commitment is made with the preparation and until his attacker takes a greater risk, which consequently enhances the chances of success of the counterattack.

ATTACKS ON THE PREPARATION

Preparation is any movement that a fencer may make to facilitate the development of his offensive action. To attack on the preparation is to attack at the moment the opponent is executing any of these movements. However, it must be done before the opponent launches his own attack.

Preparations include advances, actions with the blade, and combinations of both foot and blade action. Attack on the preparation necessitates selecting the best moment that the opponent is off balance, unable to react promptly, and consequently unable to protect himself immediately. Attacks on the preparation must not be complex, which would allow the opponent time to reorganize himself. A simple attack, preceded whenever possible with an attack on the blade or a taking-of-the-blade, and compound attacks incorporating only one feint are most effective.

The attack on the opponent's advance should be started the moment he moves the front foot and should be in process before his foot lands on the ground. If during the advance there is blade contact, a beat or pressure preceding the attack will increase the chances of success. If the blades are not in contact, one should proceed with a feint, followed by a cutover or disengage.

Against opponents who move smoothly with well-controlled footwork, it is difficult to select the right moment to attack on their advance. One should concentrate on attacking their blade preparation, for example at the time of engagement or change of engagement. A simple attack is usually sufficient, whether or not it is proceeded with an attack on the blade. It can be done by deceiving the engagement or the change of engagement. The beat or pressure, when used, should be done at the same time the blades come into contact to accentuate the delay in the opponent's reflex reaction.

When the opponent is using multiple feints, an attack with taking-of-the-blade is effective. This must be done while the feint is moving forward to avoid a possible dérobement. Croisé or sometimes opposition is very effective.

If the attack on the preparation can be made when the opponent advances to have a blade engagement or while making his feints, the chances of surprising with the attack are even greater.

Analysis

The opportunity to develop a successful attack is best when the opponent is preparing his attack—for example: when he engages the blade, tries to gain the right distance, makes an attack on the blade, feints with an arm incompletely extended or without threatening the target, and so on. The chances to attack successfully depend greatly on the mechanical execution of these actions by the opponent. Fencers very often perform actions that are meaningless or "motions without intention." They are neither prepared to attack nor, even less, to defend themselves because they rely on their reflexes or instinct rather than on tactics and strategy.

To attack on the preparation requires a total evaluation of the opponent's game so that one can almost anticipate his every move. It must be executed *before* the opponent starts his own attack. If done when the opponent's attack has already begun, the action is a *counterattack*. There is only a split second, therefore, during which the attack on the preparation can be made. For instance: When an opponent constantly seeks a blade engagement, the tactic is to lead him into his own distance of attack and either to deceive his engagement with a disengage or compound attack (one-two or double, depending on his expected defensive move) or at the instant the blades make contact to attack the blade (beat or pressure), followed immediately by a simple or compound attack.

When the opponent proceeds with false attacks without a definite plan or simply as a mechanical reflex action, again lead him into the right range, then execute an attack preceded by a beat or pressure on his blade. The attack on the opponent's blade should be made *while* it is progressing with the false attack. There is always the possibility that the opponent is preparing for a second-intention action. If so, it should not take too long to discover his strategy and deal with it accordingly by using either the appropriate compound attack (based on his defensive moves) or the counter riposte if his intention is to parry and riposte your attack.

BOUTING

Scoring a hit in fencing can be accomplished in different ways. The best way is to surprise the opponent with a swift attack executed with one motion —a *simple attack.* If the opponent is defending himself well, a more complicated action, a *compound attack,* should be used. This involves a *feint* to draw a reaction from the opponent and then acting upon it to reach the target. If one does not succeed with the attack, or if the opponent is quicker in developing the attack, then one should rely on a defensive move called a *parry.* A parry blocks the opponent's attack and subsequently allows a return attack called a *riposte.* When the opponent makes wide motions while attacking, an experienced fencer will not use a parry but instead will stop his opponent's action at its inception by using a *counterattack.*

This is the basic repertoire of actions a fencer should acquire to be able to bout with some chance of success. At a higher level of fencing, however, tactics and more subtle actions are needed. For instance, *second intention* in foil, *counter time* in epee, or *finta in tempo* in sabre are a must in the repertoire of any fencer of top caliber.

The following is by no means a complete synopsis nor the formula for invincibility. It is intended as a comprehensive way of classifying some types of fencers and also some types of games in order to help fencers develop a tactical game.

In former times fencers were not permitted to engage in bouts until they had reached a high level of development in their technique. It was common for young fencers to take two or more years of lessons as preparation. They were learning the "how" before the "why" of fencing actions.

Though this classical method certainly developed skill, the time demand on the students was so great that it discouraged many promising beginners. And it was soon found that the development of technique was not impaired if one experienced bouting at an early stage. Although a progression of exercises is necessary before fencers can engage in bouting, it is not unusual for fencers to face an opponent after a few months of fencing lessons. Naturally, the better technique the fencer has at the beginning, the more chance he has to score. But the development of technique is pursued today by a parallel progression of experience in bouting.

"How" an attack is being made is becoming somewhat secondary (which does not mean that it is unnecessary!) to "why" a specific attack would be more successful than another, or "why" a certain tactic would be more appropriate against a specific game, or "why" an action has so specific a meaning. However, beginners should not start bouting until they are able to execute correctly the basic simple and compound attacks and the corresponding defensive moves.

To score, a fencer learns at the beginning to use the different attacks he can execute with a fair chance of success. Starting with simple attacks, he will resort to compound attacks only when the first one is not successful.

While executing the simple attack, the fencer also tries to notice the kind of parry used by his opponent and under which conditions. In this way, although his attack may have failed, important information is being gathered that will be useful at the next opportunity.

Keen observation, therefore, is a quality that must be stressed to the beginner. Successful tactics cannot be developed unless a fencer learns to mentally register the opponent's different reactions under specific circumstances.

A successful attack requires the following:

1. The right distance, which can be attained only through footwork and practice.

2. The right strategy, based on observation.

3. The right moment to attack, or timing, which requires trained reflexes and constant judgment and decision.

When to make the attack is usually the most difficult decision in bouting. A fencer should attack:

1. When his opponent is not ready. For instance: (a) when dropping his arm unconsciously or due to fatigue; (b) when recovering from an attack without being prepared to defend himself.

2. When the opponent is making a preparation either: (a) with the blade: engagements or feints; (b) while advancing to gain the proper distance for his attack; or (c) with the blade while advancing.

The factors that help timing or selection of the moment to attack will be either the opponent's blade or leg motion or the tempo of execution. The fencer should be familiar with both aspects. Both sensory perception and tactile sense are important in fencing.

An advanced fencer has a wide repertoire of actions from which to choose. A clear understanding of the basic tactical concepts will allow him to select the successful attack or defensive move.

At the beginning of a bout a period of observation is important, particularly if fencers are facing each other for the first time. The height of the opponent gives some indication of his reach and consequently of the distance to be kept. His en-garde position very often reflects whether he is a forceful and nervous fencer or a calm and well-controlled opponent.

If the opponent's footwork is smooth and the blade motions are well controlled, it indicates an advanced level of technique. Consequently, normal reactions can be expected against specific attacks or preparations and the issue of the bout will most likely be determined by the tactics employed. If the opponent's footwork is jumpy or uneven and the blade motions are wide, one should be wary, for his blade can come from any direction. Consequently, a safe distance should be kept until more information is gathered. In the meantime, the tactics should be either to parry at the very last moment, when the attack is reaching the end of its trajectory or its momentum or to counterattack at the very beginning of the attack. Never attack until a pattern of the opponent's reactions has been established.

Analyses of Specific Types of Fencers

The following analyses of some types of fencers are broken down into two parts:

1. A description of the fencer's game, which represents the basic game the type of fencer should try to develop.

2. The defense against the particular type of game described, representing one tactical answer that is possible (but not exclusive of other answers). This knowledge may, of course, be utilized by both the attacker and defender in planning their overall strategies.

The Short Fencer.   A short fencer must make preparations to gain the distance of attack. He usually proceeds his attack with quick footwork (advance or retreat). He tries to control his opponent's blade whenever the opportunity presents itself and uses advance-lunge or balestra with his attacks. If the blade is not easily captured, he proceeds with quick feints to keep pressure on his opponent and prepares his attack without running the risk of being counterattacked. Against a taller opponent he tries to use second intention or to attack him on his recovery. He tries to close in at the end of his attack to deny his opponent the opportunity to riposte. His retreat is rapid so as to reach a safe distance quickly. His parry and riposte are very rapid and usually delivered with a lunge or a half-lunge. He uses counterattack once in a while, depending on his opponent's technique, but most of the time relies on his defense.

Against a short fencer keeping the right distance is the important element, for he has to develop his attack from a close distance. Once the distance has been evaluated, be prepared to vary parries and counterattacks to make it difficult for him to pin down your reactions. This will slow down his tempo and pace. The tendency for a short fencer to look for the opponent's blade before attacking comes from his need for security while making his attack. Therefore, do not hesitate to feed him the blade while being ready to counterattack or counter disengage on his change of engagement. Attack on his preparation by using cutover, one-two, and so on. The use of false attacks is very effective in keeping him at a safe distance and serves as a preparation for second intention. The idea is to induce him to parry and riposte while being ready to parry his riposte and hit with a counter riposte. Avoid close combat in which he has a decided advantage and greater experience.

The Tall Fencer.   A tall fencer usually has a slower tempo than a short fencer. This does not mean that he is not as fast as a short fencer. The tall fencer tries to impose his slower tempo during a bout and uses counterattacks to take advantage of his reach. He especially tries to attack his opponent on his preparation with simple or compound attacks, but without complexity. He uses the remise sometimes rather than the redoublement. As his recovery is slightly slower, he is wary of being attacked on his recovery. Consequently, he is often prepared to use the stop thrust while recovering. Because of his long arm and the difficulty of riposting at a very close range, he tries to keep a long distance to overcome this defect.

The basic tactics against a tall fencer are the following:

1. Gain the distance by using quick footwork combined with rapid feints to put him off balance.

2. Gain control of the blade before developing the attack by using attacks on the blade or taking-of-the-blade to get the right-of-way or gain a safe tempo when executing the attack.

3. Give preference to second intention by provoking counterattacks on the part of the tall fencer which can then be parried and riposted, or to false attacks to provoke a parry and riposte which in turn can be parried and counter riposted. However, this requires a deep commitment with the false attack and a corresponding element of risk.

4. Attacks on his preparation. These are the safest and most successful ways to score if they are executed without hesitation and carried all the way to completion.

EPEE

The epee in present competitions is a direct descendant of the dueling sword used until the beginning of the twentieth century. The difference is that the point, rather than being sharp, is blunted and covered with a safety device.

From the beginning of the seventeenth century the foil had been the "learning" weapon for those who intended to become "spadassins" or "mousquetaires" or simply considered fencing an excellent discipline to be included in the educational curriculum. Through the centuries, however, foil became more restrictive as to which part of the body was to be considered a valid target, as to when an attack had the right-of-way, and so on.

The foil game became very different from the reality of a real combat. At the end of the nineteenth century, many duelists, relying too much on their foil technique and forgetting that the important matter in a duel was to hit *without* being hit in return, lost out to epee fencers who had specialized in that weapon.

There followed an inevitable conflict between those who believed that foil training was necessary to become a good duelist and those who believed that a foil fencer had no chance against an epee fencer in a real combat. From then on epee became a weapon with its own characteristics and technique, all derived from the reality of the duel.

Time and distance, in terms of *when* the attack was delivered and *which* part of the body it had touched, became the deciding factors in competitions. Needless to say, the task of judging winners became extremely difficult and resulted in complaints and bickering by competitors over the judges' decisions.

Some fencers decided that the only way to resolve the problem was to use an electric apparatus that would register every touch on the target. In 1936 electric signaling was officially adopted by the International Fencing Federation.

With the electric system, the concept of epee drifted further away from the reality of combat to become a sport in which speed rather than self-protection was the basic objective. It became a matter of hitting the opponent 1/20th of a second before he could score. Thus, simple actions were emphasized over more complex ones, as in foil.

This does not mean that epee fencing does not require as much technique as for other weapons. One should remember also that although the target seems to be easier to reach because it includes the entire body, it also offers the same advantage to the opponent.

EQUIPMENT

The uniform requirements are the same in epee as for the other weapons. It must offer total safety for the fencer. The material used must be strong enough to resist penetration. The epee jacket must also have a groin strap.

The epee is the heaviest of all three weapons. The blade is triangular in cross section, with a groove in the middle. In the electrical epee blade, the wire runs down the groove from the point to the connector inside the guard. The guard of the epee is much larger than in foil—5 5/8 inches in diameter—and curved to give protection to the hand.

The rigidity of the blade is an important factor, so much so that it is subject to strict regulations by the International Fencing Federation. A too-flexible blade is not recommended, for too often in a forceful action the bend given to the blade sometimes allows a late counterattack to score, thereby producing a double hit.

The handle and pommel are the same as in foil. Modern fencers tend to use the pistol grip in epee. It gives more power to offensive or defensive actions and enables the fencer to resist the opponent's attack on the blade. However, power should not be emphasized to the detriment of point accuracy and variety in the repertoire of one's game.

GRIP

The pistol grip, which fits the hand of the fencer, does not need to be described. What follows concerns the French handle.

The epee is held with the groove in the blade facing upward. The lower part of the handle lies on the second phalange of the index finger. The thumb is on top of the handle and the tip of the thumb about one inch from the guard. The other three fingers wrap around the handle, ready to sustain the action of the first two. Since the weapon is heavier than the foil, a tighter grip is required. The advantage of the French grip is that an experienced fencer can use it to gain an advantage in length by holding the handle closer to the pommel. This grip may be particularly advantageous for fencers using a game of dérobement. On the other hand, such a grip is vulnerable (too weak) against fencers who use constant attacks on the blade. In this case, the fencer should return to the previously described hold of the weapon— for example: with the thumb close to the guard.

As in foil, the thumb and the index finger control and guide the point.

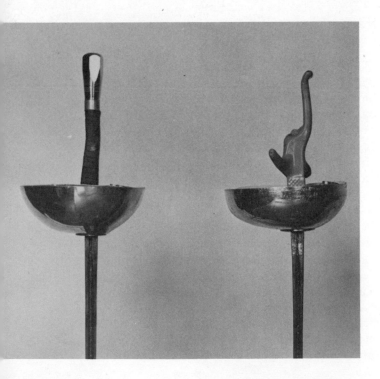

French and pistol grips

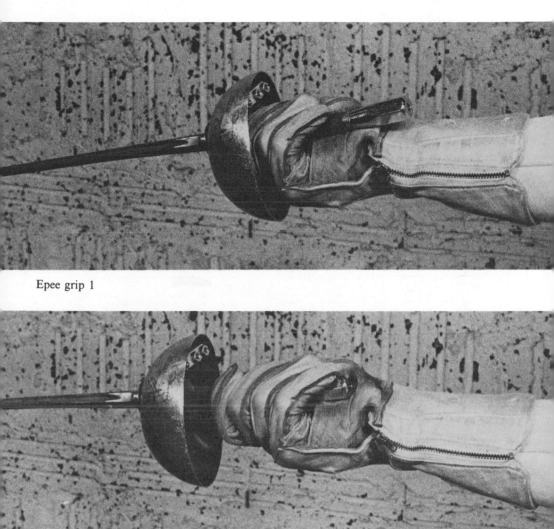

Epee grip 1

Epee grip 2

TARGET

The target in epee includes the entire body, front and back, from the tip of the toes to the top of the mask! The combination of this all-inclusive target and the "no-convention" rule, which allows only the time factor to determine who hits first, give epee fencing the characteristics of dueling.

Epee target

LINES

Although the target in epee is considerably more extensive than in foil, the concept of lines applies equally in epee, since it concerns the portions of space, in relation to the target, within which the hand can move.

However, because of the characteristics of epee fencing, some hand positions or parries that have specific purposes in protecting specific lines in foil do not serve the same ones in epee. For example: Against an attack to the foot, the parries of septime or octave, which are the corresponding defensive moves against attack in the low line in foil, cannot succeed. This is because the opponent's blade going in a trajectory aimed at the floor makes either parry useless. The only recourse against an attack to the foot is to move the foot out of reach at the time of the attack and/or counterattack the opponent's action.

Due to the "right-of-way" convention in foil, the fencer does not have to protect himself against the opponent's remise when riposting after making a successful quarte parry if the riposte is executed immediately following the parry (and scores a hit). In epee, however, the quarte parry must be taken far out of line to afford the necessary protection against an almost systematic remise or counterattack by the opponent. Usually the remise done in time arrives ahead of the uncovered riposte. This advantage is used very often by epee fencers. Consequently, a few hand positions either are not recommended or should be taken with some modifications adapted to epee fencing in relation to their respective lines.

The lines to be considered for the purposes of teaching and better understanding will still be the same as in foil: inside line, outside line, high line, and low line.

HAND POSITIONS

The need to protect against attack to the forearm requires that the epee fencer keep himself well protected with his guard up at all times. To afford this protection, positions with the hand in supination (palm up) should be used in preference to positions with the hand in pronation (palm down).

Sixte Position

The hand is in supination, at a level horizontal with the elbow, the arm more extended (about three-quarters) than in foil. The guard is to the right, the main purpose being to protect against attack to the outside line of the forearm and body. The point of the blade is slightly above the horizontal and directed toward the opponent's target.

Octave Position

The hand is in supination, to the right as in sixte, but the point of the blade is lower than the hand. The arm is three-quarters extended with the forearm in a horizontal position.

Seconde Position

The blade position is the same as in octave, but the hand is in pronation and consequently may offer the opponent an easy target for attacks to the open hand and forearm. Seconde can be used as a defensive move, but it is relatively easy to deceive and should not be repeated too often.

Tierce, quarte, septime, and prime are not very safe positions, for they offer too much uncovered arm target. However, they can be used as defensive moves with the appropriate blade opposition while maintaining hold of the opponent's blade. These parries should be used judiciously as they tend to trigger an immediate and automatic remise or counterattack on the part of the opponent.

EN-GARDE POSITION

The en-garde position in epee is extremely important, for it must serve a supplementary purpose to that in its use with other weapons. It must offer protection to a larger target—the entire body. Basically, the en-garde position in epee reflects a defensive-offensive rather than a strictly offensive position.

Since the arm, head, and knee are part of the target, the stance should be shorter than in foil so as to keep these parts of the target well protected behind the point of the weapon. The knees should be bent so as to allow fluency in the footwork and spontaneity in the lunging actions.

The arm should be three-quarters to fully extended without being stiff, the elbow relaxed so as to allow freedom of movement in offensive as well as defensive actions. The hand should be in supination, the point of the weapon lower than the hand and directed toward the opponent's guard.

The body should be erect with the weight of the body slightly on the front leg. The left arm, as in foil, is raised in an arched position, the elbow at shoulder level, the hand with fingers relaxed and open, falling over the wrist.

En-garde position (side)

En-garde position (front)

Analysis

The en-garde position must be adapted to the physical qualities of the fencer. A tall fencer needs to lean slightly forward so as to facilitate the lunge, while a short fencer needs all the power from his back leg to carry on the attack. What must be remembered is that the weight of the body should be divided in between the two legs so that it does not impair the smoothhness of the footwork.

Too much weight on the back foot makes the retreat difficult while delaying the beginning of the lunge. Too much weight on the front foot may be a good position from which to start a fleche. However, such a position tends to give the lunge a downward direction, thus limiting any further actions if needed after an attack fails.

Finally, the hand in supination offers the best possible protection of the arm behind the guard, while being extremely important for developing point accuracy. With the hand in supination the point can be controlled easily, as lateral movements are very limited while there is practically no limit or effort required to execute vertical motions.

THE LUNGE

The maximum spontaneity, speed, and length of the lunge is determined by the quality of the en-garde position and depends on the fencer's training and natural attributes.

The lunge in epee tends to be neglected. The reason perhaps comes from the philosophical approach of many fencers—"Either I hit or I get hit"—thus keeping their game at a primary level and denying themselves the opportunity to develop a more complete game. The target in epee is divided into three sections based on nearness or distance from the opponent: (a) the forearm; (b) the knee, biceps, and head; and (c) the body. Accordingly, the required length of the lunge depends on the distance of the target to be reached. To keep the right distance, a fencer needs to control his lunge—to be aware of his maximum reach.

To execute the lunge with the arm fully extended, project the leading foot forward with the heel skimming the floor and to such a distance that once the foot reaches the floor, the front knee is situated vertically above the middle of the foot. The projection is combined with a sharp stretching of the back leg, while at the same time the left arm is brought snappily to a position parallel to the back leg. The back foot should be firmly flat on the floor during the whole process. The trunk of the body is kept as erect as possible, thus keeping one's own target as far away as possible from the opponent's point.

The Recovery

From the lunging position the recovery is made again through leg action and not by muscle effort from the back of the torso as many fencers tend to do. To recover backward, flex the back knee while pushing backward from the heel of the front foot. The left arm is brought snappily back to its original position in the en garde, while the front foot is replaced in the original en-garde position.

To recover forward, the action starts with a slight shift forward of the body weight, the front knee pointing over the toes, helped by a push from the back foot. The latter is then brought forward to the proper distance from the front foot by flexing the back leg.

Analysis

Since epee has no conventions, it allows fencers to take advantage of every opportunity to score. The opportunity can be evaluated in terms of speed (hit 1/20th of a second ahead of the opponent) or in terms of an opened target, or it can be judged through the difference in reach between the two opponents. For all these reasons, the lunge (and the fleche) should be executed with maximum safety in mind, the target being well protected behind one's own point. The trunk of the body should be kept as straight as possible to maintain a maximum distance from the opponent's point. Recovery from the lunge, if an attack fails, necessitating immediate withdrawal from an exposed position, is delayed if the lunge is badly executed. Similarly, it is impossible to recover with the sword arm fully extended if the weight of the body has been shifted too much to the front leg. In any event, the accuracy of the point is greatly reduced.

A fast recovery places the fencer out of reach or allows for a subsequent offensive action when the attack has failed. Sometimes it is advisable to recover with the feet coming close together to gain a greater margin of distance while keeping the arm fully extended with the point threatening the opponent's target.

FOOTWORK

Advance (The same footwork described in the foil section can be used in epee.)

To advance, move the front foot forward about one to one and a half feet, then bring the back foot up at an equal distance, keeping the feet flat on the floor to be in the position to develop an attack if the opportunity occurs or to retreat immediately if the opponent attacks. The reverse procedure can be used in advancing and is particularly useful in epee. The back foot is moved first, close to the front foot, then the front foot is either moved forward an equal distance or the lunging action is started if the conditions for attacking are favorable. A combination of the two methods of advancing is essential for developing a good epee game.

1

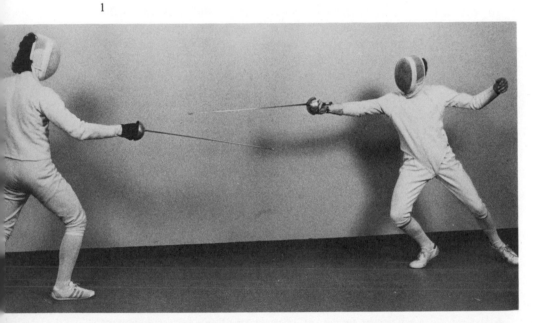

Fleche

2

3

4

Retreat

The classical way to retreat is to move the rear foot backward about one foot, the front foot following immediately to resume the en-garde position. The reverse action, the front foot moving first, then the back foot following the proper distance, has the advantage of removing the front part of the target without delay.

Passe Avant and Passe Arrière

The passe avant and passe arrière, described in the foil section, can also be used, but cautiously. When the fencer executes them he is slightly off balance. This moment can be used by his opponent to start an offensive action. Thus, the passe avant and passe arrière should be done only at a safe distance.

Analysis

Distance is paramount to a successful epee game. Mobility requires special attention and depends on the quality and variety of footwork. Constant training to improve footwork technique is essential. The footwork learned for foil is valid in epee, but the consequences of not keeping the right distance in epee are more severe than in foil. A heavier weapon, the epee does not permit, in most instances, a rapid enough defensive move when the opponent launches a surprise attack.

The validity of the remise against the riposte (unless the latter is executed with opposition) and the possibility of being counterattacked any time the target is left open demands that the proper distance always be kept. Epee fencers should particularly work at perfecting advances and retreats that correspondingly allow them to gain the distance to develop an attack without giving warning to their opponent or allow them quickly to withdraw the threatened target out of reach of the opponent's attack. To attack, the advance is made by moving the back foot close to the front foot and then lunging immediately while the opponent is still at the right distance. To retreat, the front foot is moved first while the fencer counterattacks into the opponent's attack.

Break in tempo is extremely important in gaining the distance of attack without alerting the opponent. It also helps to confuse the opponent in his evaluation of his distance. Keeping the same tempo makes it easy for an experienced fencer to anticipate a forthcoming attack and to act appropriately. A break in tempo with footwork reflects a break in tempo with the point motion.

DEFENSE

The defensive system in epee is directly related to the quality of the en-garde position. It then seems logical that defense becomes the next concern in the learning of epee technique.

There is no convention in epee, only the difference in time (and consequently of length) between the hits of two fencers matters. The defensive system should be concentrated on allowing the "achievement" of these differences.

GUARD OPPOSITION

The en-garde position and the parries require that the sword arm be almost constantly extended. If, in the en-garde position, the weapon is held as described in the section on "Grip," a simple opposition with the guard of the epee will offer total protection against an attack aimed at the forearm. This opposition requires a very small displacement executed with the arm or wrist to stop or deflect the opponent's point. It does not exclude the use of the counterattack. Rather, the combination of both constitutes the basis of the epee game.

The arm target may be divided into four sections: inside; outside; upper part; and lower part—all defining the different sides of the arm in the en-garde position.

Against an attack aimed at the inside forearm, the guard is moved by pointing the heel of the hand an inch or two toward the left. The extent of the opposition depends on the angle from which the opponent's point is coming at the target. However, the epee fencer should refrain from making

Guard opposition as a defensive move against an attack to the forearm wide motions in opposing the guard to the oncoming point for that would open the arm target on the opposite side, a situation that could be exploited by the opponent at the next opportunity.

Against an attack aimed at the outside, a proper en-garde position should require no extra movement for protection.

Attacks to the upper part of the forearm require a slight bending of the wrist with the heel of the hand moving upward. Against an attack aimed at the lower part of the forearm, the guard is moved downward.

This defensive game based on opposition with the guard is valid only against classical attacks to the forearm. Another form of attack, called "dig," often renders opposition practically useless. Against this type of attack a different tactic is necessary.

PARRIES

When opposition is insufficient to stop the opponent's point, the parry must be used. Although every parry described in the foil chapter has an application in epee, some are not recommended, for they do not offer sufficient protection against a remise or continuation or require a too-wide displacement of the arm to guarantee protection to the arm.

Again, as there is no convention in epee, the parry must fulfill a dual purpose: total protection while allowing the opportunity to riposte with success. Nothing is more frustrating to a beginner than to execute a good parry and riposte and be hit in the process. This is one reason why the parry should be made with the arm extended and moving forward into the opponent's attack.

Sixte

Sixte from the classical en-garde position (point lower than the hand) is executed by simply raising the point toward the opponent's blade, then opposing the strong part of the blade to the weak part of the opponent's blade. This is done by slightly raising the guard and the arm while maintaining the initial opposition of the guard to the right until completion of the riposte. In the process, the arm is fully extended and the legs are ready to accompany the point motion with a lunge or part-lunge, depending on the distance. Opposing with the strong part of the blade and the guard strengthens the defensive move and deflects the opponent's point. This is especially needed when the opponent has a strong or stiff arm. If the blades are already engaged in the sixte position, the sixte parry requires only the use of the strong part of the blade and opposition with the guard.

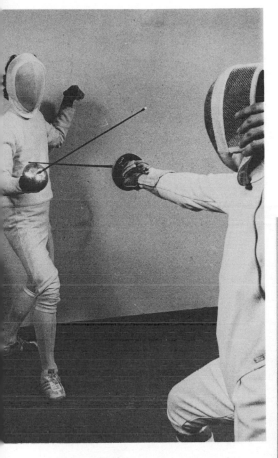

Sixte parry

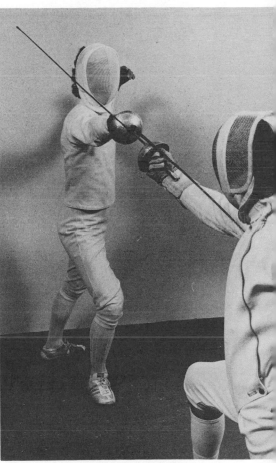

Counter Sixte

This parry is executed by doing a circular clockwise motion with the point passing under the opponent's blade and in the process picking up the opponent's blade from the inside to move it to the outside. Here, too, it is essential to use the strong part of the blade against the weak part of the opponent's blade and also to cover one's own target with opposition from the guard. While doing the counter sixte, use the minimum displacement of the forearm to avoid a counterattack or dérobement on the part of the opponent.

Sixte parry and riposte with opposition

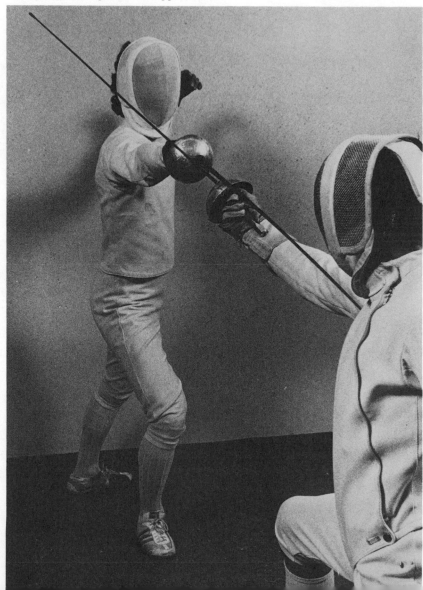

Octave

From sixte position, octave is executed with a semicircular defensive action, which deflects an opponent's attack aimed at the target low line (body or knees). It is a very effective defensive move, which can be used sometimes instead of counter sixte, inducing more variety in the defensive system of an epee fencer. It also allows ripostes on target, which are difficult

Octave parry and riposte

 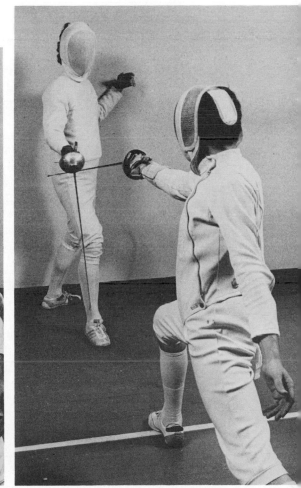

to protect. For example: riposte either to the knee, or to the inside body target without releasing contact with the opponent's blade; or riposte with a simple disengage to the biceps.

Counter Octave

From octave position, this parry is executed with the point describing a circle by passing over the opponent's blade. It has the same characteristics as the parry of octave.

Seconde and Counter Seconde

(Executed the same way as octave and counter octave except that the hand position is in pronation.)

Other Parries

The following parries are of less practical use in epee for they require either that the hand be brought out of line to offer sufficient safety, or that during their execution too much forearm target becomes uncovered:

Quarte From the en-garde position the point is raised above the guard level while the hand moves left in a lateral motion. In the process, the opponent's blade is deflected to the left. It is essential to control the opponent's blade without releasing contact and to oppose sufficiently with the guard to avoid a possible remise from the opponent. Opposition must be constantly maintained while executing the riposte. Because safety requires that the quarte position be taken out of the usual line, quarte parry is not as commonly used in epee as in foil.

Septime From the en-garde position, the point is moved down and to the left in a scooping motion. The hand and blade move simultaneously toward septime position, picking up the opponent's blade in the process. The arm is fully extended and the point kept lower than the hand. Septime is a strong parry that may be used in some cases to disconcert the opponent or when the opponent uses mostly fleches with his attacks. In the latter, it allows a quick riposte while the opponent is no longer in a position to remise. If used without discernment, however, septime has the same weakness as the quarte parry.

Prime Prime parry is not really recommended and should be used only in exceptional cases against opposition attack from the opponent. The position does not allow either a fast or accurate riposte. It requires quite a bit of training to use it effectively.

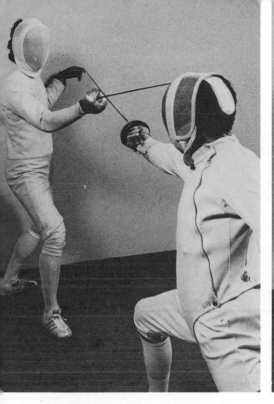

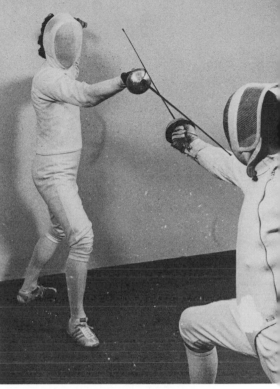

Quarte parry 1

2

Quarte parry and riposte with opposition

Yielding Parry

The yielding parry is more effective and useful in epee than in any other weapon. It is executed against opponents who attack with a taking-of-the-blade (opposition or bind). To execute it, keep the arm extended and let the opponent come as deeply as possible in the execution of his action. Then, at the last moment, roll the blade over his blade by moving the guard down to the opposite side from that in which the blades were initially in contact, at the same time opposing with the strong part of the blade and raising the point high in the direction of the opponent. The motion downward is to the right or the left depending on the type of taking-of-the-blade used by the opponent.

For example: Against the bind from quarte to octave (or seconde), which is the one most utilized in epee, the yielding parry is executed by moving the guard down very deeply and to the left while the point is raised and aimed at the opponent's chest. The opposition with the strong part of the blade is maintained constantly to avoid a possible remise or continuation to the knee.

In most cases it is not necessary to extend the arm to reach the target, as the opponent practically moves himself against the point. However, it is imperative never to lose contact with the opponent's blade. Some fencers accompany the yielding parry with a deep bending of the knees to accentuate the protective aspect of the parry and to place the point at such an angle that the opponent cannot avoid being hit.

Against a taking of the blade with sixte opposition, the yielding parry is prime. The process is the reverse of the previous one. The rolling motion is done under the opponent's blade and the guard brought up instead of down on the other side. The opponent's blade is deflected to the left by using a lateral movement with the strong part of the blade while the arm is extended to the left.

The only practical riposte is the straight one executed by accentuating the hand pronation in the prime position, thus raising the point toward the target. The point is then pushed forward in a stabbing manner while keeping contact with the opponent's blade. To give better direction to the riposte some fencers execute almost a half-turn to the left with their body at the time of the parry.

The yielding parry requires long training and a good "feeling of the blade" to be used effectively.

OFFENSE

The *simple attack* is an offensive action executed with one point motion, is directed toward any part of the body, and is executed with the lunge or the fleche.

Straight Thrust

This action is executed by extending the sword arm, hand in supination, the point aiming at the target, the lunge following immediately. During the execution of this attack, the hand should be well protected behind the guard and the guard opposed toward the opponent's point so as to avoid being hit in a possible counterattack. The attack may be directed at any of the three sections of the target.

The Disengage

In the disengage the point is moved from one side of the opponent's blade to the opposite side by passing the point under the blade while the arm is fully extended, the blade motion followed immediately by the lunge.

Straight thrust

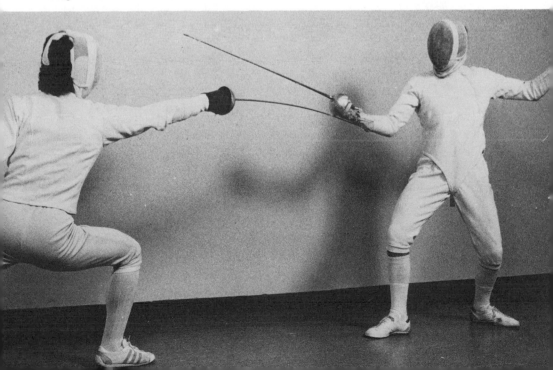

The Cutover

The cutover, executed by passing the blade over the opponent's point, is not recommended in epee. It leaves most of the forearm open during its execution while giving ample warning to the opponent, thereby allowing him either to get out of reach or to counterattack.

Attacks to the Forearm

The classical attacks to the forearm follow the same principle of guard opposition as described in the defensive system. The guard during the execution of the attack is directed, usually with a very slight motion, toward the opponent's point in order to protect one's own forearm against a counterattack by the opponent. The attack to the inside forearm is made with the arm completely extended, the point aiming at the opponent's inside target and the guard slightly to the left with the hand in supination. Against a tall fencer the arm level should be raised appropriately to protect the upper part of the forearm. Against a shorter fencer the reverse may be necessary.

An attack to the outside is executed with the arm fully extended, the guard slightly to the right with the point aiming at the opponent's outside target.

In the attack to the top of the forearm, the arm is fully extended with the guard opposing in the direction of the opponent's blade, the point aimed at the upper part of the opponent's forearm.

To attack the lower line of the forearm the guard is opposing in the direction of the opponent's blade, but with the point aiming at the lower part of the opponent's forearm.

The disengagement is possible when there is a previous engagement of the blades. The same conditions of arm and guard opposition as in the straight thrust prevail in the disengagement.

The Dig

Against a fencer whose en-garde position offers total protection to his forearm, it is extremely difficult to score with the classical attacks described above. A different approach in executing these simple attacks is necessary.

The concept of protection through guard position during the execution of the attack is disregarded and replaced by moving the forearm target away from the opponent's point. In this instance safety is attained by displacing the target area and placing it out of reach of the opponent's counterattack. The arm and the blade form an obtuse angle while executing the attack. In

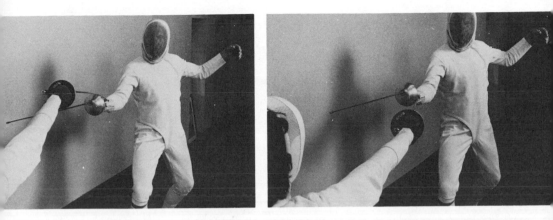

Attacks to the forearm

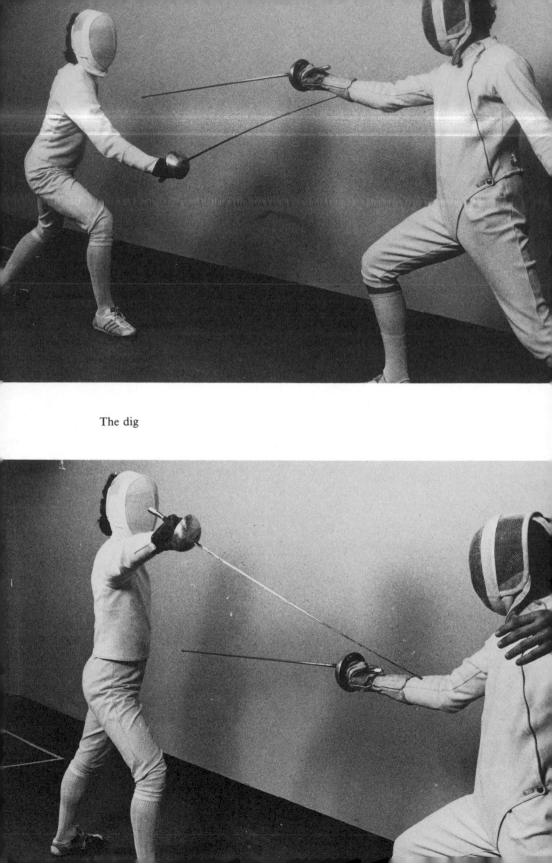

The dig

some instances the hand is turned in complete pronation to reach the target with the point hitting at the proper angle.

The dig is usually done with a sharp one-tempo movement followed with a quick recovery to avoid any succeeding action on the part of the opponent and to resume safe distance immediately. If the attack misses, there is very little recourse against the opponent's counteroffensive. The dig requires great accuracy and is usually aimed at the forearm. The angle of arm and blade required to execute the dig considerably reduce the fencer's reach, making it almost impossible to reach the opponent's body target safely.

Attacks to Other Targets

Simple attacks to the knee or the foot give an occasional opportunity to score, particularly when the opponent is unaware of his en-garde position, which places his front foot too far forward, or bends his knee exaggeratedly, because of the body leaning forward. The straight thrust or low disengage is executed in this instance in a throwing motion, with the arm fully extended, the hand in supination, and maximum speed. Immediate recovery is essential, during which the arm should be kept fully extended in the high line. Surprise is essential for success in scoring with these attacks. Therefore, they should be used judiciously and from the right distance.

Simple attacks to the body are easy to parry and are not recommended. Attacks to the biceps are preferable. They require careful preparation and usually the use of the fleche. A simple attack to the body has a better chance of succeeding when preceded by an attack on the blade or a taking-of-the-blade, thus denying the opponent the opportunity to counterattack early.

COMPOUND ATTACKS

A compound attack is an offensive action that includes one or more feints before the final movement. The feint can be simple or compound and takes the name of the attack it resembles.

Feint of simple attack is made with either a straight feint or disengage feint. Feint of compound attack can be a one-two feint . . . ; double feint . . . ; or straight feint, disengage feint. . . . The final action is intended either for the forearm; the biceps, knee, or head; or the body.

Examples of compound attack with a simple feint: straight feint to outside forearm, disengage to under or to inside of forearm, or knee, or foot. Straight feint to under forearm, disengage to biceps.

Examples of compound attack with a compound feint: one-two feint to outside forearm, disengage to under forearm. Double feint to under forearm, disengage to biceps (either inside or outside).

Analysis

There are four purposes of the feint:
1. To get an opening.
2. To provoke a withdrawal of the arm on the part of the opponent.
3. To provoke an extension of the arm.
4. To induce the opponent to parry. Consequently, the feint in a compound attack requires more or less penetration depending on the kind of reaction one wishes and the target that the final action is aimed at hitting.

To be meaningful the feint must ensure a progression of the point toward the target, or progressive penetration with every feint. Penetration is most effectively achieved with advances or a half-lunge, the final action being executed with either a lunge or a fleche. Because of the possibility of counterattack and the longer distance usually kept between epee fencers, most feints are aimed at the forearm or biceps area (although a feint to the knee or the foot can be useful if not used too frequently).

Attack to the Body

Tactically, an attack to the body should be used only sparingly and will have a better chance of succeeding under the following three conditions:

1. When the opponent is in the process of withdrawing the arm.
2. When the opponent is in the process of extending the arm.
3. When the opponent is reacting to feints with parrying movements.

Whenever possible the attack should be aimed in line with the biceps so that the point in some instances may reach this part of the target first.

To elaborate on condition (1) above, there are two instances in which the opponent may withdraw his arm:

(a) The opponent withdraws his arm naturally, without being influenced by any oncoming threat. For instance: when recovering from an offensive action which has failed.

(b) The withdrawal is a reaction to a threatening point. For instance: reacting to a feint to the forearm.

It is up to the fencer to observe which of these cases prevails and to use the appropriate attack at the first opportunity presented. It is necessary to anticipate the withdrawing of the arm if the attack is to succeed. Anticipation is necessary to catch the opponent off balance while he is withdrawing his arm and before he can settle himself and respond to the situation.

When feints are necessary, they should be executed with sufficient penetration to induce the proper reaction and also to be in the best position to deliver the final action from the right distance.

Example of an attack to the body: deep feint to under forearm to make opponent withdraw his arm, then disengage to the body (or biceps) with a fleche. Opposition with the blade and guard is recommended, as is keeping the hand in supination.

In condition (2) above, against an opponent who fences with his arm fully extended, the best tactic to use is attacks made with taking-of-the-blade. However, as the fully extended arm is typically the position of a fencer who relies on counterattack and dérobement, it is imperative that some preparations be made before the final action. The preparations should aim at playing on the opponent's reactions so as to be able to set up either the moment of the attack or the specific conditions leading to the final action.

For example: through pressure and/or blade engagement, force the opponent to deceive or execute a disengagement while he keeps his arm extended. Proceed forward with the preparations to make the opponent change the direction of his disengagements a few times. Then suddenly take his blade in the expected line with a sixte or counter sixte (depending on whether the opponent's blade is in the inside or outside line) with a strong opposition. The attack is then carried to the body, usually with an advance-lunge or a fleche. In either case, the final attack has to be done in one tempo and without hesitation so as not to give the opponent time to adjust the distance or execute a defensive move. The bind can be used equally well under these conditions and requires the same kind of preparation as that described above for opposition.

In condition (3) above, when the opponent tends to react with a parry in response to specific feints, one should play into the opponent's reactions and attack the body while deceiving his parry. In order to succeed, a fleche should be used, at least with the final offensive movement. For instance: feint to the inside biceps with an advance; when the opponent parries counter sixte, deceive the counter sixte while executing the fleche. When attacking to the body there is always the possibility of a counterattack from the opponent. It is then necessary either to make deep penetration with a cautious approach or to play on an immediate reaction on his part by means of a sharp feint to his open line.

PREPARATION OF ATTACKS

Because of the distance and the blade position maintained by two fencers, there are fewer opportunities to execute an *attack on the blade* than in foil. Besides, it cannot serve the purpose of gaining the right-of-way, since this does not exist in epee. However, an attack on the blade can be useful in epee either to delay the opponent's reaction, provoke a reaction, or create an open target such as the forearm.

There are three attacks on the blade, the same as in foil:

The Beat

This can be a light tap or a strong beat against the opponent's blade. It should be executed with the minimum displacement of the hand to avoid uncovering one's own target. Because of the position of the blades, one should be careful to look for the perpendicularity of blades to get the maximum result when executing the beat. Depending on the position of the opponent's point, the beat is most commonly used in quarte, sixte, septime, and seconde. In some instances it may be useful to slightly rotate the wrist to give more sharpness to the action.

The attack following the beat is generally executed immediately to take advantage of the opponent's reaction. The arm should be completely extended at the end of the beat action. When the purpose of the beat is to force an opening of the target, it should be done with a strong and sharp impact to displace the opponent's point and allow a time advantage over his reaction. If the purpose of the beat is to avoid provoking a counteroffensive reaction by the opponent, the beat should be done lightly. For instance: when the opponent is unaware of his own open target or of his vulnerability in some target area (knee or foot), the beat attack should be done in one quick tempo, with the arm practically "shooting" toward the target. The beat can serve other purposes too, such as disrupting the opponent's tactics or concentration, tiring his hand, and so on. When a counterattack is expected, the beat then serves as a preparation for a second-intention action.

The Pressure

As in foil, the pressure is a quick-blade, springlike action more or less accentuated, executed through finger and wrist motion. The pressure does not hold the opponent's blade, but is intended to make him react with a counter pressure. Its purpose is to take advantage of the reaction by executing a disengage attack to the forearm or the knee. The pressure serves other purposes, such as provoking a counterattack or forcing the opponent to uncover part of his forearm target. As a counterattack usually comes at the end of the pressure reaction, this attack on the blade should be executed with the arm fully extended to preserve the initial time advantage.

The pressure can also be used as a preparation for second intention.

The Expulsion

This is described in the foil chapter. It requires a strong wrist and forearm motion and is usually followed by a straight thrust to the forearm or biceps. The expulsion can be used against an opponent who keeps his blade in a horizontal position (not necessarily with the arm fully extended). It is most effective against an opponent holding his weapon without much firmness. However, the expulsion is easy to deceive and tends to carry the point way out of line.

Analysis

In most instances attacks on the blade produce a time advantage that must be exploited immediately to be successful. They require that the arm be almost, if not completely, extended to minimize the distance the point must travel so the time advantage is not lost.

When the opponent does not react to any attack on the blade, it is most likely that his basic game is to counterattack at the opportune moment. In this case, the attacks on the blade should be used as preparation for second intention, which necessitate the use of taking-of-the-blade actions.

The best defense against attacks on the blade is to learn not to react and to be prepared to counterattack at *the time* of the beat and *not as a reaction* to it, when the opponent's attack is expected. Avoid giving the opponent the opportunity to execute an attack on the blade by not presenting one's own blade in the appropriate position. Evading the opponent's attack on the blade is also useful and should be executed as often as possible with a counterattack to capitalize on the moment of surprise that generally follows.

ATTACKS WITH TAKING-OF-THE-BLADE

As mentioned in the foil chapter under preparation of attack, the purpose of taking-of-the-blade is to control the opponent's blade until completion of the final action. This is an extremely desirable condition, since it affords safety in epee while scoring a hit. Taking-of-the-blade requires some preparation, for it is executed mechanically and without judgment and can be evaded or counterattacked by the opponent.

Opposition

The only safe oppositions are the ones executed either in sixte or octave (or eventually seconde). The opposition takes the opponent's blade in one line and controls it until the completion of the action. It is executed with the strong part of the blade against the weak part of the opponent's blade to give a firm holding and better leverage. At no time should the opponent's blade be released, for most likely he will instinctively counterattack.

Bind

This blade action takes the opponent's blade from a high line and brings it to the opposite diagonal low line. For example: from quarte to octave, or sixte to septime. Conversely it can be done from a low line to the opposite high line. However, this kind of bind offers more danger as the hand must be uncovered when going into the septime position, and the bind of octave to quarte requires a wide opposition in quarte to provide protection against

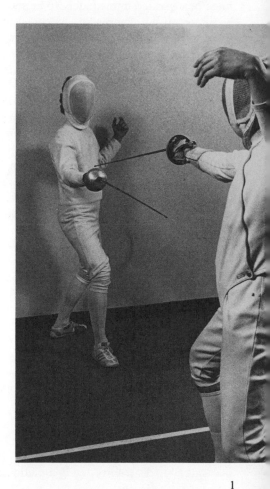

Bind in quarte

a counterattack or dérobement. As specified for the opposition, the use of the strong part of the blade against the weak part of the opponent's blade is essential.

Croisé

This is very effective, particularly against fencers using the remise indiscriminately. It takes the opponent's blade from a high line to the corresponding low line on the same side. It can be done also in the reverse, from low to high. However, because of the safety factor, the only valid croisés used in epee are the croisé from quarte to septime and from sixte to octave, and these are especially recommended when riposting.

2   3

Croisé

1

Envelopment

This consists of taking the opponent's blade in one line and, through a circular motion executed without releasing the opponent's blade, bringing it back into the same line. In the process, the point is moved forward toward the opponent's target.

Analysis

Taking-of-the-blade actions are particularly useful in epee. During their execution the point should progress toward the target and they should be made without hesitation or releasing the hold on the opponent's blade at

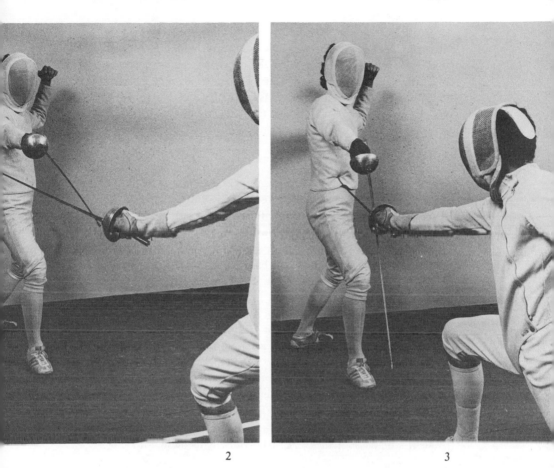

2   3

any time. To be successful, taking-of-the-blade has to surprise as well as be
carefully planned.

Preparations of the attack can also be used in second intention by provoking the opponent's counterattack with a feint of taking the blade, and using
a second taking-of-the-blade for the final hit. For instance: execute the
beginning of the quarte croisé with an advance to make the opponent
counterattack into the high line. Then immediately seize his blade with a
sixte opposition, which will be carried to the forearm or the body with either
a lunge or a fleche.

The use of distance and timing are necessary to surprise and to avoid any
unexpected reaction from the opponent.

In most instances, taking-of-the-blade requires the use of an advance lunge or fleche in order to reach the target, which is usually the trunk or the legs. However, the bind and the croisé can be used as a defensive move —particularly the croisé in sixte or quarte—against fencers who use the opposite hand (left-hander against right-hander or vice versa).

COUNTERATTACKS

The counterattack in epee is an offensive action executed against the opponent's attack in order to score 1/20th of a second ahead of him. (The 1/20th of a second is the time allowed before the electrical circuit in the scoring machine shuts itself off when a hit has been registered. When the two fencers score within this lapse of time, it becomes a double hit.)

Owing to the time lapse and based on the lack of conventions in epee, the counterattack is a basic part of the defensive-offensive system of every epee fencer. It may be executed in three different ways:

1. With a simple extension of the arm and opposition with the guard offering protection against the opponent's attack.

2. With a dig, the effectiveness of which depends on withdrawing the target from the opponent's point and at the same time counterattacking with a hooking-arm motion, usually to the opponent's forearm.

3. With a dérobement (evasion), by doing a disengage into the opponent's preparation either when the blades are in contact or by evading the opponent's blade as it seeks to make the engagement.

Basically every opponent's attack (simple or compound) aimed at the forearm should be counterattacked instead of parried. Parrying an attack to the forearm offers too many opportunities for the opponent to score. For instance: The parry can be deceived or even evaded at the last moment. A counterattack can be made during the riposte succeeding the parry. A remise can be executed immediately into the parry motion.

The classical en-garde position, with the point aiming at the opponent's hand and the guard protecting the forearm, requires a simple extension of the arm in the execution of a counterattack. It is a quick action, offering much safety. It allows selection of the moment to counterattack whenever the opponent leaves his arm uncovered. The counterattack can be executed at the beginning of the opponent's attack (including preparations, if any), during, or at the end of his attack. Against simple or compound attacks intended for the forearm, use of the counterattack depends on timing and the availability of open target.

Whenever the opponent's attack offers few target openings, the dig can be used to reach behind the opponent's guard. The angulation with the weapon and the displacement of target create conditions that usually surprise the opponent. The dig can be successful against attacks to the body. It requires excellent point accuracy and selection of the right moment to counterattack. If the dig misses the target, there is usually little time to retreat or make another defensive move.

When the opponent uses a great deal of preparation (attacks on the blade or taking-of-the-blade), there is sometimes advantage in playing into his game by feeding him the blade, then counterattacking at the right moment with a dérobement (evasion), usually a disengage.

Analysis

The counterattack is an extremely effective action in epee. Some fencers develop a game based exclusively on counterattack. Such a game, of course, is limited and requires extreme patience. In any event, the counterattack requires excellent timing, a precise evaluation of distance, and a very accurate point.

The classical counterattack is by far the safest for it offers protection with the guard as well as the opportunity to continue with another action (offensive or defensive), which the dig rarely permits. The dérobement requires a good "feel of the blade" and excellent finger work to move the point at the right moment.

A good epee fencer should be able to execute the different forms of counterattack to be able to choose the appropriate one to the circumstances presented.

A special mention should be made about the dig in the counterattack actions. Contrary to the classic attack, the dig gives little protection during its execution. The effectiveness of the dig comes from the following:

1. Displacing one's own target to make the opponent's attack miss.

2. Hitting with such an angulation of the blade that it is practically impossible for the opponent to parry to ward off the blade.

3. Aiming at the forearm while the opponent is forced either to aim for the body or to realign his point to hit a target.

The dig requires great arm speed and an excellent sense of distance and timing. If it misses it usually offers no recourse to a safety defensive move except a quick retreat. Left-handers have a natural ability for the dig.

Once a fencer becomes successful with the dig he tends to base his game almost exclusively on this action. This type of game is easily recognized and a good fencer should be prepared to use the correct tactics against it.

The fencer using a dig usually does not react much to preparations, waiting only for the definite attack to be launched. In this case, it is important to keep pressing while gaining the distance that will allow a final attack to the biceps or the body. A false attack followed by a redoublement is the most effective way.

The same principle may be applied to reach the opponent's forearm. Since he will try to withdraw the arm and body target, one should make the final action in one quick tempo with opposition of the guard. A false attack to provoke the dig, then a quick replacement of the point to the opponent's forearm is effective. If the dig is expected in a specific area, it is necessary to use a wider-than-usual opposition with the guard.

The other tactic is to provoke the opponent's dig, then to attack him when he recovers from it. This requires perfect timing. It is called counter stop.

VARIETY OF ATTACKS

The types of attack includes three different actions:

1. The *redoublement* consists of doing a second attack immediately following a recovery (forward or backward) from an unsuccessful first attack. In epee, however, most redoublements are used with a recovery forward. They are safer than the fleche and are usually effective for pursuing an opponent who retreats automatically from most offensive actions. The redoublement can also be used after a riposte when the opponent manages to withdraw out of distance after his unsuccessful attack.

2. The *reprise* is usually made with a disengage from the lunging position and immediately following an unsuccessful attack. It is effective against a fencer who does not riposte (or counterattack) and is not aware of the close distance.

3. The *remise* is the most used and successful of all three types of attack. It consists of replacing the point immediately on the opponent's target after one's attack has failed. To be successful, it requires that the point be close to the opponent's target at the end of the initial attack to take advantage of the time factor and the shorter distance traveled by one's point as compared to that of the opponent.

The remise can be done effectively following either an attack or a riposte, or even a counterattack that has failed. It should be executed systematically against an opponent who either parries without riposting or parries without sufficiently covering his target; or in a close combat situation when it is too dangerous to try to break away.

The best defense against the remise is to break the distance after the opponent's unsuccessful attack. Against a fencer who remises almost instinctively, however, a taking-of-the-blade (opposition, bind, or croisé), which will control the opponent's blade until completion of the action, is better strategy for it allows a safe defense and the possibility of scoring at the same time.

COUNTER TIME AND COUNTER STOP

The counter time in epee can take two forms:

(1) the classical one, which is an offensive action executed after having parried the opponent's counterattack; and

(2) the counter stop, which consists of timing the opponent's counterattack and counterattacking his action in return, either with a dig or by making the counter stop with guard opposition, thus deflecting the opponent's point.

Counterattack

The counter time

In epee the counterattack usually is intended to hit the forearm. Therefore, the distance considerations for counter time are different from that in foil. In epee usually a greater distance is involved, permitting the use of actions made with taking-of-the-blade. Particularly effective are the opposition, the croisé, and the bind. The envelopment can also be used but requires a more complex movement, limiting the surprise and speed that is essential in epee. The greater distance in most cases requires the use of the lunge or fleche in carrying out counter time. As an example: advance with a beat feint to the forearm; when the opponent counterattacks, take his blade with a bind from quarte to seconde while lunging (or fleching) at once to the body or the knee.

The counter stop

By its very concept it needs excellent timing and consequently presents some risks. When used judiciously, however, it is very disturbing to the opponent, who tends to feel unsafe at every stage of his attack.

The best defense against a counter time is basically the remise or the dérobement. However, the parry, and particularly the yielding parry against the bind, is also very successful.

BOUTING

Epee fencing as compared to foil has no conventions such as the "right-of-way." The valid target has no limitation and includes the entire body. Consequently, epee bouting offers more opportunity to score while reducing the value of the parry, which is so essential in foil and sabre. However, the possibility of being counterattacked at any time during the execution of an attack removes all security, which in many cases is provided through the right-of-way in foil.

Although most actions used in foil are valid in epee, the very concept of epee requires that some actions be used with caution (for example: compound attacks), while others (like the counterattack), which are often risky in foil, are part of the basic strategy in epee. Because of the above considerations, the following principles should be applied:

Offense

1. Attacks to the forearm will be made by simple attacks, directly or preceded by an attack on the blade. Compound attacks can be used if the

opponent reacts to feint or beat actions with a defensive move. However, the opponent may counterattack or extend his arm rapidly at any time during the execution of one's attack. Thus, attacks should surprise the opponent and be carried out with speed, precision, and timing. No visible muscular preparation should warn the opponent of the oncoming attack. Before using a beat attack, the opponent's reaction should be tested to (a) find the open target; (b) discover his reaction—for example: counterattack, withdrawal of the arm, defensive move; and (c) determine if there is a delay in his reaction. If there is a delay in his reaction, proceed with a simple attack to the open target. If the opponent's guard already offers an open target, no beat or only a light beat may be necessary to avoid triggering his counterattack. On the other hand, a strong beat may be necessary to bring the opponent's point out of line and thus create an open target. Against a fencer who reacts to a beat with a counterattack or by withdrawing his arm, the use of second intention, as described in attacks to the body, is recommended. If the opponent reacts with a defensive move, continuation of the attack with reprise or deception is most effective.

2. Attacks to the body require the use of second intention for safety and gain the 1/20th of a second advantage necessary to score over the opponent's hit. The object of second intention is to use the opponent's predictable reactions under specific circumstances and to act upon them. For instance: When the opponent reacts automatically to a beat on his blade by making a counterattack, the strategy is to provoke a counterattack and to immediately take over his blade with a taking-of-the-blade (either a bind or opposition). An opponent with advanced technique is aware of this possibility and will try to be in a position to deceive the taking-of-the-blade. The next step then is to make the opponent react after a succession of quick preparations so that the final taking-of-the-blade will surprise him in a direction he did not expect or by involving him with succeeding actions so that he cannot deceive the final one. Some preparations may induce the opponent to withdraw his arm. In this instance the preparation for the second intention includes false attacks followed automatically by a continuation of the attack to the forearm or the body at the same time the opponent withdraws his arm. The continuation can be executed either with a recovery and lunge or balestra or a fleche.

Defense

The system of defense one has to employ depends largely on the opponent's reactions and one's repertoire of actions, but one should remember these general rules:

1. Always be aware of the opponent's distance of attack and prevent him from coming into that distance.

2. Against attack to the forearm, a simple opposition with the guard is best. When conditions are favorable, the defensive move should be accomplished with a counterattack into the opponent's attack. Since the difference in reach between two fencers is negligible when the target is the forearm, most counterattacks should be directed as close as possible to the target near the guard to avoid a possible double hit. The counterattack should be followed immediately by a retreat or in some instances with a remise.

3. Attacks intended for the biceps or the body either should be counterattacked, if the opponent presents an open target at the beginning (or the end), or parried and riposted if the counterattack presents too much risk.

The parry is recommended almost exclusively against attacks by the opponent to the body. The riposte subsequently delivered should be executed without releasing contact with the opponent's blade until completion of the action.

A good fencer should be able to use the following parries with equal dexterity and efficiency:

(a) Sixte opposition against an opponent's attack aiming at the outside line.

(b) Octave (or seconde) against an attack aimed at the low line.

(c) Counter sixte (or counter octave, depending on the position of the blades at the commencement of the attack) against an opponent's attack intended for the inside line.

(d) Quarte parry, which should be used with caution and with sufficient opposition to prevent the opponent's remise, which is always possible and almost instinctively developed among some fencers. In this case, the blade should be taken way out of line and not released until completion of the riposte.

When the opponent uses taking-of-the-blade as his basic game, dérobement (evasion) is the most efficient tactic. It can be executed at the moment of blade contact or without contact. It is usually followed by a quick retreat to step out of reach.

Against a fencer who is not too accurate with his counterattack or parries and either does not riposte or delays the riposte, the remise is extremely successful. The replacement of the point should be done automatically, and with a dig, if necessary. The remise can be equally successful when following a riposte or a counterattack that either has been parried by the opponent or has missed the target. The advantage of the remise is that the point is already very close to the target area and consequently must be moved only a short distance (requiring less time) to score.

SABRE

Modern sabre fencing had its origin in the cavalry sabre used in the seventeenth century. While duels were fought with rapier or epee among Western Europeans, the cavalry sabre was the dueling weapon in Hungary. Italians, whose temperament seems particularly suited to fencing, had a strong influence in the development of the game from the sixteenth century on. Most prominent in foil and epee, they also left their imprint on the development of the sabre.

Although a Hungarian fencing master, Josef Kersztessy (1810–1872), the "father" of Hungarian sabre fencing, had modified considerably the technique of handling the sabre during the nineteenth century, the method of modern sabre fencing was strongly influenced by an Italian fencing master, Giuseppe Radaelli. He established new principles based on simple, fast moves with a minimum of wrist action. The use of a light-weight sabre undoubtedly favored the development of the new technique.

Later, a few Italian fencing masters, and particularly Italo Santelli, influenced the development of Hungarian sabre champions. These included his son, Giorgio, who following in his father's footsteps is developing American champions in New York.

However, the Hungarians are credited with the development of modern sabre fencing because of the creation of a Hungarian school of fencing masters after the First World War. The result was a revolutionary sabre technique based on blade control through finger action and the simplification of the defensive system. The consequences were a complete domination by Hungary in the sabre competitions of the Olympic Games from 1908 to 1964* in which they won both the Individual and Team events. In 1964 in Tokyo the Soviet Union, a rapidly rising country in the sport of fencing, succeeded for the first time in taking the Olympic Sabre Team title away from Hungary.

WEAPON

The sabre is both a thrusting and a cutting weapon; a hit can be scored either with the point or with the two edges of the blade. One edge is represented by the total length of the front part of the blade, and the other edge by the back part of the blade comprised of one-third of the length from the tip. The sabre blade, like other weapons, is made up of a strong part (near the guard), a middle part, and a weak part (close to the tip). Each part is about one-third of the length of the blade. Made of steel, it has a T-shaped cross section, which is reduced in size progressively from its base to the weak part of the blade. It then assumes a rectangular cross section for the remainder of its length, ending in a blunted point.

Hits allowed with back edge

Hits allowed with entire leading edge of sabre

*In the World Championships in 1959, Poland won the Sabre Team title.

The *guard* is made of steel or aluminum alloy. It has a convex form with a knuckle bow and is wide enough to offer protection for the hand.

The *handle* is similar to the French foil handle, except that the different curves are intended to fit into the palm while holding the weapon in an almost vertical position. It is made of wood or plastic, covered with rubber, cord, or leather. Orthopedic handles or pistol grips, as in foil, are practically nonexistent in sabre. Some modifications to accentuate the curves have been tried, but without offering any special benefit for the grip.

The *pommel* is much smaller and lighter than that used in foil, but offering the appropriate counterweight to the blade.

TARGET

The target consists of the trunk of the body (front and back) located above an imaginary horizontal line passing through the points formed by the two hips and the torso when the fencer is in the en-garde position (usually about two inches below the navel) plus the arms and head.

Sabre target

LINES

The lines in sabre are defined by three sides of the vertical rectangle enclosing the valid target with the two lateral sides and the upper side covering the head. The side toward the sword arm is the *flank*. The opposite side is the *chest*. The upper side is the *head*.

When an attack is made to the flank, it is called a flank cut; to the head, head cut, and so on. A cut to the side of the head is called cheek cut (right or left), while attacks to the forearm are called outside, inside, over, or under arm cut, depending on which part of the forearm the attack lands.

GRIP

Since the sabre is mainly a cutting weapon, the grip reflects this purpose. The lower part of the handle, which is situated inside the guard, rests on the second phalange of the index. The index finger forms a groove in which the handle is inserted. The thumb is extended on top of the handle, usually without reaching the guard. The other three fingers wrap around the handle in the same manner as the index. The index is at a level about one inch below the tip of the thumb.

The weapon is held lightly and without tightness. The fingers must play freely with the weapon: the thumb and index in a pinching motion, while the other three fingers, particularly the little finger, are ready, through slight contractions, to help the action of the first two.

The thumb, directly opposite the edge of the blade, plays an essential part as the "shock absorber" in the defensive system. It presents the forward edge of the blade at the point of impact with the opponent's cutting action. In the offensive, the thumb is the "ball carrier" with the help of the index and the little finger during the execution of the final cut.

Sabre grips

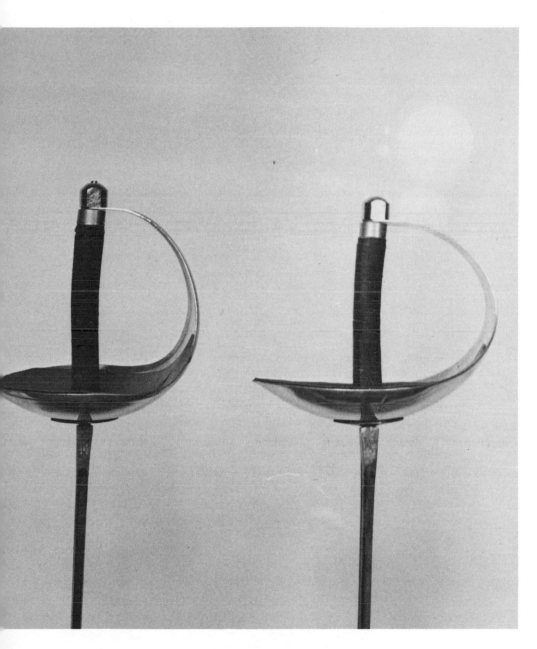

EN-GARDE POSITION

The en-garde is essentially the same as in foil, with greater emphasis on keeping the body erect, to facilitate greater mobility. A slight shift forward of the center of gravity during offensive actions may take place, and a return to the original stance will occur during defensive moves.

The left arm is not raised as in foil. The left fist is placed on the rear hip and remains there at all times, mainly to protect the arm against any cuts.

The hand holding the weapon is at a lower level than in foil, at about hip level, and on the right side. The wrist is slightly flexed outward to present the edge of the blade and the guard against any cutting attack to the flank or the forearm. The blade is held in a slightly diagonal position, the point directed toward the opponent's eyes. The torso should be kept upright with the shoulders relaxed, the knees bent, ready to start the lunge or fleche at the moment of the attack and whenever needed.

THE LUNGE

The lunge in sabre is not appreciably different from the lunge with the other weapons except that the trunk must be more erect to be in a position to execute subsequent defensive movement if the attack fails. Because of the trajectory and direction of the opponent's riposte, it would be practically impossible to execute a successful defensive move if the body is leaning exaggeratedly forward at the end of the lunge. Thus the lunge in sabre may be slightly shorter than in foil, while the fleche, allowing the fencer to reach at a farther distance, is more often used.

The recovery forward or backward requires the same technique as in foil, with particular emphasis on the speed of recovery and control of the blade in the proper hand position.

THE FLECHE

The fleche, as a means of carrying on the attack (and counterattacking the opponent), can be executed from the en-garde position or after a half-lunge.

(Note: From a full lunge the fleche loses its momentum and element of surprise because of the time delay in bringing the body forward.)

To proceed, extend the arm in the direction of the intended target, the hand lower than the shoulders, while shifting the center of gravity onto the front foot with the knees still bent. The rear foot crosses over in front of the leading foot, while the front leg propels the body toward the target. The action may be continued by a quick run. To avoid a brutal contact with the opponent, which would lead to a penalty, the attacker should pass to the side of the opponent: to the left side if the opponent is right-handed, to the right side if he is left-handed.

After an unsuccessful fleche attack, a good fencer should be able to parry the opponent's riposte. However, because of the closeness between the fencers after a fleche, there is no benefit in a returned counter riposte unless the action has been planned tactically.

The fleche presents surprise but also great risk. It should be used with discretion and judgment.

DISTANCE

Distance in sabre is slightly longer than in foil. It is practically the same as in epee, since the arm is also a valid target. The blade in the cutting action, however, comes from a wide angle. Consequently, greater distance is necessary to permit the parrying of the attack.

Three distances have to be considered in sabre:

1. Short distance, or distance of riposte.
2. Middle distance, or lunging distance.
3. Long distance, or fleching or advance-lunge distance.

FOOTWORK

Mobility is perhaps even more important in sabre than in foil and epee fencing. The manner of controlling distance and the more natural way the weapon is handled allow more freedom of movement in sabre fencing. The purpose of footwork remains the same: to gain the right distance before attacking, to stay out of reach of the opponent's attack, and to confuse the opponent about the matter of distance. The same analysis applies in sabre as with the other weapons:

1. Avoid "up and down" or body-swinging motion during footwork.
2. Keep the knees constantly bent.
3. Emphasize the jump backward as a quick way to stay out of reach when the opponent makes a fleche.

The passo avvicino is very useful to keep the proper distance while on the defensive against a fleche. Advance and retreat followed with a lunge or a fleche should be constantly drilled.

The *sliding step* with sudden stop or jump should be included in the footwork. It is highly effective in misleading the opponent about the distance, as a preparation for a subsequent fleche, or in provoking the opponent's attack (using second intention). Skimming the floor, the front foot moves slowly forward about one foot. Then a short jump is executed with both feet landing at the same time in an en-garde position, which will allow the execution of any of the above tactics.

HAND POSITIONS

Three positions of the hand constitute the basic defensive system in sabre: *tierce, quarte,* and *quinte* (third, fourth, and fifth). Two secondary positions, *prime* and *seconde* (first and second), are not used as frequently as the other three but are useful.

Tierce

Tierce is the usual hand position assumed in the en-garde position. The elbow is close to the hip, the hand to the right at a lower level than the elbow. With the wrist bent slightly outward, the weapon is held with the blade in an almost vertical position and the point directed toward the opponent's eyes and inside the target area.

Tierce position

Quarte

The hand is to the left, closer to the body than in tierce. To change from tierce to quarte, the wrist is bent inward as the forearm, rotating around the elbow, moves toward the abdomen. The blade is almost vertical, the edge in position to oppose any cutting action coming to the left side of the target.

Quarte parry

Quinte

The hand, guard, and edge of the blade are positioned upward, the weapon held on a horizontal line about a foot from the head. The hand is to the right, higher than the head, with the forearm almost vertical and the elbow slightly higher than the shoulder. The fingernails are turned forward (facing toward the opponent), the wrist bent outward.

Quinte position

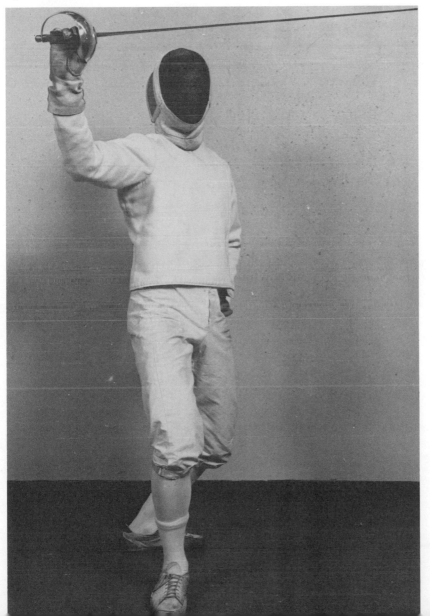

The Two Secondary Positions

Prime   The hand is to the left, the arm horizontal, thumb turned downward. The blade is in an oblique position with the point directed toward the floor and at knee level so that the edge and the guard will oppose the opponent's cut to the left side.

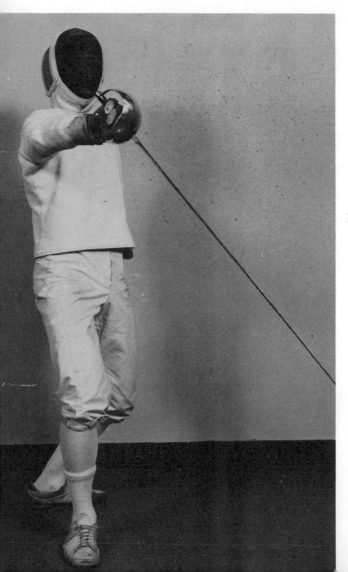

Prime position

Seconde position

Seconde   The hand is to the right and lower than in the prime position, the arm stretched, hand in pronation, and the point of the blade directed toward the opponent's knee. Blade and wrist form an angle. The edge of the blade will oppose an attack intended for the right side of the target.

Analysis

To move from one position to another, the wrist should move so that the blade edge is opposed promptly to the oncoming attack. The thumb position should be opposite the blade edge to absorb the shock of the cutting blow. Control of the point by the "pinching" action of the thumb and index is essential to ensure the right blade position. The positions must be taken with the fingers holding the handle firmly and ready to execute any actions.

SIMPLE ATTACKS

These are offensive actions executed in one tempo, with one blade motion while lunging or doing a fleche. They can be executed with the point or with a cutting action of the blade. The target to be reached determines the name of the attack.

The Head Cut

Through a slight wrist motion, present the front part of the guard and blade with the edge leading forward. The point is aimed just above the top of the opponent's mask as the arm is extended. The hit on the mask is executed by a contraction of the last three fingers as the thumb and wrist move the blade slightly downward. The lunge must be executed at the same time as the arm is stretched toward the opponent—both in a one-tempo action.

Head cut

Head cut with the fleche

The Flank Cut

From the tierce position, rotate the wrist to complete pronation (palm down), bringing the front of the guard and the blade edge in a position parallel to the floor. The cutting edge is directed toward the opponent's flank as the arm is extended. During the action the hand should be at such a level (usually just below the shoulder) that the forearm is not exposed to a stop cut (counterattack). The hand should be to the right and blade and arm form an open angle.

The Chest Cut

While moving the hand forward, rotate the wrist to bring the blade in the direction of the chest. The hand is in supination (palm up) and ready to execute a slashing motion at the hit. The hitting motion should be made by contracting the fingers and rotating the wrist in a circular motion, bringing the blade back into the tierce hand position.

The attack to the right cheek is executed in the same manner as the attack to the flank, except that the blade is directed toward the right side of the head. Therefore, the point should be slightly higher when threatening the target.

Chest cut   1   2

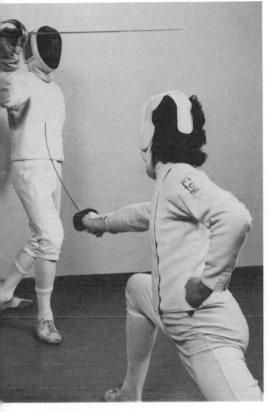

3

4

The Belly Cut

The attack to the belly follows the same characteristic as the attack to the chest except that the cut is aimed at the waist. The belly cut requires a deeper quarte parry to be effectively blocked. Consequently, this attack is preferred to the chest cut.

The Arm Cut

The cutting action to the arm requires the same technique as the cutting action to the body. For example: A cut to the right side of the forearm is similar to the flank cut; the cut under the forearm is similar in execution. A cut to the left side of the forearm requires the same finger and wrist motion as that for the chest cut; the cut to over the arm employs a similar execution (with a blocking action of the blade at the time of the hit).

The right side of the forearm is called the *outside;* the left side the *inside;* the upper part of the forearm *over;* and the lower part of the forearm *under.*

Cheek cut

Stop cut counterattack to
the forearm (outside)

Stop cut to the underarm

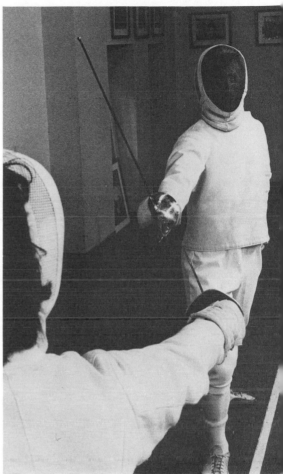

Making a direct attack to the forearm requires one of the following two conditions: (1) either that the opponent keeps his forearm exposed or (2) that the fencer succeeds in getting his opponent to react and subsequently to expose his forearm. The limited target of the forearm and the very slight motion of the guard or the blade required to protect it make the attack to the forearm more difficult to execute than the attack to the body. However, the chance to hit is greater when the forearm cut is used against an opponent who exposes his forearm when starting his attack or during its execution.

In these latter instances, the cut is considered a counterattack and the arm cut becomes a *stop cut*. To be allowed, the stop cut must reach the target one tempo ahead of the attacker's final action.

Attack with the Point

From the en-garde position, the fencer extends the arm while rotating the hand in pronation. The blade is horizontal with the point aiming at the target. The hand should be above shoulder level and enough to the right that the guard protects the outside forearm. The arm and blade should form an obtuse angle.

The point attack can be simple, with a straight thrust or a disengage; or compound, with a one-two (deceiving a lateral parry) or a double (deceiving a circular parry).

Although direct attacks with the point are not overly recommended because they can be easily parried, a combination cut and point attack can be very successful. Examples: flank feint and disengage (point), or disengage

Point thrust   1

2

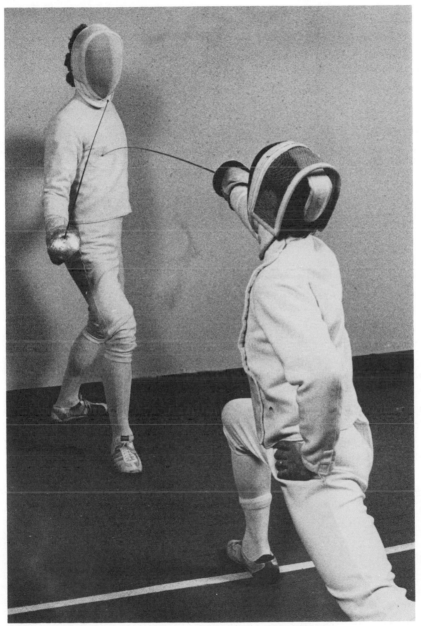

feint (point) and cut to the flank. Simple attacks require distance, timing, and speed.

Analysis

In sabre, the hit must land before the leading foot in the lunge reaches the floor, so the arm must be extended *with* the lunge. These are two reasons: (1) The distance in sabre is greater than in foil and (2) the angle of the blade in sabre makes it easy to see which part of the target the opponent's blade seeks. If the arm is extended before the lunge, it signals the opponent, who then easily parries the attack.

Correct execution of the different simple attacks is essential—without it, precision and blade control would suffer.

To develop a correct technique, the simple attacks should be executed first with the arm only—at short distance (riposte); then with the lunge— middle distance; and finally at long distance with advance and lunge or fleche. The finger action is particularly important at the moment of the hit, and exercise to develop blade control through the fingers is particularly recommended in the beginning. The final cut to the target must be executed by contraction of the fingers combined with a slight flicking of the wrist.

During execution, the hand and guard position require special attention to properly offer protection against counterattack at the forearm. The front edge of the blade, through slight wrist rotation, should always be presented to the opponent's open target. The guard should be at a level where the front part always protects the hand and forearm against a counterattack.

Surprise increases the chance of success and is particularly possible when the opponent cannot sustain an attack (for example: when he is too involved in preparing his own attack or is making preparation). The situation occurs upon an opponent's mistake or by forcing the opponent to err through footwork, break of tempo, and so on. The chance for a successful attack also increases if it is made when the opponent advances (making his preparation), relaxes his guard position, after recovery, and so on.

In the recovery the bending of the sword arm should be gradual to achieve the best defensive position. The blade should be in a diagonal position to permit a quick parry or to be ready for a counteroffensive against the opponent's attack.

PARRIES

The parry is a defensive move intended to block the opponent's attack. The defensive system is based on three basic and two secondary positions.

Parry with the Three Basic Positions

To parry quarte from tierce position: Rotate the wrist inward to present the edge of the blade toward the oncoming attack. The blade takes an almost vertical position with the point moving slightly out of line. The hand moves laterally, closer to the body than in the tierce position, to completely guard against a belly cut.

To parry quarte from quinte position: The wrist is rotated downward with the hand executing a diagonal motion to reach quarte position as described above. The point of the blade moves a minimum distance in the process.

Quarte protects against: attack to the chest or belly; attack to the forearm; and attack made with the point, ending in the inside line.

To parry tierce from quarte position: Quickly bend the wrist outward and follow with a side motion of the hand to tierce position. The blade is presented vertically with the point slightly out of line. The front edge of the blade and the thumb should oppose the impact of the opponent's attack.

Parry with the Two Secondary Positions

To parry seconde from quinte position: The blade is moved diagonally with the point moving slightly ahead and outward, while the hand moves slightly to assume the seconde position. The edge of the blade and thumb must be in the correct position to avoid a possible disarmament.

To parry seconde from tierce position: The blade is moved down in a semivertical motion as the wrist turns into complete pronation (palm down).

To parry seconde from prime position: The blade moves with a lateral motion while the elbow slightly bends to assume the seconde position. The wrist remains bent outward.

Seconde protects against: attack to the flank.

To parry prime: This parry is usually taken from tierce or seconde position in a sweeping motion.

To parry prime from tierce position (from the quinte position, the principle is basically the same): The point is brought down quickly in a downward curve. The blade is then moved with a diagonal motion as the hand takes the prime position.

To parry prime from seconde position: The blade is moved with a side motion with the hand going from seconde to prime while maintaining the same outward angle of the wrist.

Prime protects against: attacks to the chest or belly and to the inside forearm.

To parry tierce from quinte position: The wrist is kept bent outward and the blade comes to a vertical position as the hand is brought down into tierce as described above. The elbow is closer to the waist for safety.

Tierce protects against: point attack to the outside and attack to the flank and outside forearm.

To parry quinte from tierce position: Quickly move the point toward the left as the hand moves vertically with thumb and edge of the blade facing upward and wrist maintaining the same outward angle. The final position of the blade is horizontal. Quinte also can be executed with a sweeping motion by the point executing a counter tierce-like movement before the blade assumes its horizontal position.

To parry quinte from quarte position: The point of the blade requires very little motion, while the wrist is bent outward. At the same time, the hand moves in a diagonal direction to the quinte position as described above.

Quinte protects against: cutting attacks to the head and point attack. When used against point attacks, it can be performed with a flying parry-riposte combination. The hand and blade should move at the same time.

Analysis

As mentioned in the section on hand positions, when moving from one position to another the motion must start with a wrist rotation so that the edge of the blade promptly opposes the oncoming attack. The thumb opposite the edge plays a "shock absorber" role. The defensive move should halt as soon as the attack is blocked. If not, it gives an extra push to the opponent's blade, a mistake too often and intuitively made by beginners. The parry is a "closing" rather than a "slamming" action. When done with a beat, control of the opponent's blade is even more important to ensure an accurate riposte.

The parry should be taken with the strong part of the blade, offering maximum resistance to the opponent's blow. The blade should be in a vertical position to offer the greatest protection to the target.

Depending on the distance and tactical intent, the parry can be taken with the arm in a normally bent position or three-quarters extended. If the arm is bent, it reflects the fencer's intent to parry at the end of the opponent's attack. It indicates a fencer who is confident of his defensive reactions. If the arm is extended three-quarters, the fencer should keep his own target as far away as possible from his opponent's attacks. This position will probably lead to more use of the counterattack.

Combining short and long arm positions with the parries is recommended to ease adjustment to tactical demands. However, in some instances it may be a necessity because of the difference in height between two opponents.

In any event, it is essential to block the attacking blade with finger action at the moment of parry to allow an accurate and immediate riposte. It is also important for the elbow to be relaxed during the parry to allow for maximum force in the succeeding action.

RIPOSTE AND COUNTER RIPOSTE

As in foil, the riposte and counter riposte are offensive actions that follow a successful parry. The statements in this section concerning the riposte apply equally to the counter riposte.

Head parry and riposte to flank

The riposte may be simple or compound. It is simple when executed with one blade or point motion. It is compound when there is more than one blade or point motion.

The riposte can follow the parry *immediately* or with a *delayed* tempo.

The simple riposte can be executed either with a cutting action or with the point on the side where the parry has taken place. It is then called a *direct riposte*. For instance, from the tierce parry the riposte can be executed either with a head cut, flank cut, cheek cut, forearm cut, or a point thrust. Which to use depends on which part of the target offers the best opening and how quickly the opponent can protect a specific area.

Similarly, the simple riposte is *indirect* when executed either with a cutting action or with the point on a different side from that of the parry. For example: From a tierce parry, the riposte can be directed either to the

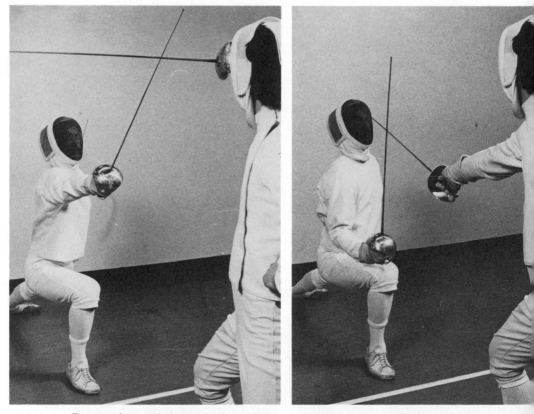

Parry quinte and riposte to the head

Prime parry and riposte to the head

chest or the belly, or with a point disengage to the body. If the opponent reacts strongly when his attack has been parried from a tierce position, an immediate riposte to the head and cut to the inside forearm can be executed as an indirect riposte.

The compound riposte requires extremely good control of the blade and perfect knowledge of the opponent's reactions. This is necessary because the compound riposte is susceptible to counterattack and a possible remise on the part of the opponent.

The riposte and counter riposte can be executed from the en-garde position with an advance, a lunge, a fleche, and an advance and lunge or fleche.

Riposte and Indirect Riposte

Parry necessitated by final movement of the attack	Direct riposte to	Indirect riposte to
Tierce	Head Outside forearm Right cheek Point thrust	Belly or chest Head Disengage point
Quarte	Head Right or left cheek Chest or belly Inside forearm Point thrust	Flank
Quinte	Forearm Flank Point thrust	Head Chest or belly Inside forearm
Seconde	Outside forearm Right cheek Flank	Point thrust inside (kind of bind) Point thrust after cutover in low line
Prime	Under forearm Point thrust Flank	Head Chest or belly

The part of the body designated in the chart signifies that the riposte has been executed with a cutting action.

The riposte with a delayed tempo takes advantage of the opponent's immediate reaction after his unsuccessful attack. The riposte is not deliv-

ered immediately after the parry but delayed until the opponent has practically completed his withdrawal (with his arm or with a recovery).

Analysis

In foil, as in epee, the only way to score a hit is with the point. Consequently, the blade's trajectory is always practically horizontal or perpendicular to the target. In sabre, the angle of the blade actions makes it easier
to defend the target. Consequently, it is more difficult to riposte without
meeting the opponent's blade on the way to the target.

To develop a successful defensive game, a fencer must learn to riposte to
all the different target areas and from all the different parry positions to
capitalize on every opportunity to score. The opponent quickly detects a
defensive game limited to the same type of parry and riposte and then easily
finds the appropriate tactic for a quick score.

The importance of finger action in holding the weapon has been emphasized. Through contraction and relaxation they allow blade and point control, which is essential for parry and in delivering an accurate and successful
riposte. Remember that the thumb and index are the guiding fingers, while
the other fingers support the first two, adding strength when needed.

At the moment of parry, the grip must be firm without being tight, or
the riposte may be delivered with insufficient blade control and a slight
delay. During the riposte the fingers should direct the blade toward the
target without impeding arm motion and vice versa.

In some instances the riposte will not necessitate a fully extended arm,
particularly if the coming attack is made with a fleche or with a balestra,
which brings the fencers to a very close range. Trying to extend the arm
at too close a distance invariably results in the riposte missing the target or
landing on the opponent's blade.

In the compound riposte, at close range, the first feint should be made
with a guard-like motion rather than with the blade, and the arm should
not be fully extended, to prevent overshooting the target at the final hit.

The riposte with a lunge or fleche is most useful against fencers who
recover or withdraw very quickly after developing their attack. However,
there is always the possibility of being counterattacked during the riposte
if the forearm is left open, or after the riposte if a poorly executed parry
shows the opponent an open target.

COMPOUND ATTACKS

The same definition of the compound attack in foil applies in sabre. The
compound attack uses one or more feints during an attack. The feint is made

with either the point or the cutting edge. The feint itself can be simple
or compound, depending on the tactic required to make the opponent
react.

The purpose of the feint is to simulate an attack and trigger a reaction
(defensive or counteroffensive) from the opponent. Usually the feint is made
with the arm fully extended (only in a few instances with the arm bent).

Following is a general classification of compound attacks, including one
feint, which can be executed from the en-garde position with a lunge,
advance-lunge, or fleche:

With Cutting Action Only

The feint aims at the body, with the final hit ending on the body. Example: head feint, then cut to flank. The opponent parries either quinte or
quarte.

The feint aims at the body, with the final action ending on the forearm.
Example: chest feint, then cut to the outside forearm. The opponent parries
either quarte or prime.

The feint aims at the forearm, with the final hit ending on the body.
Example: feint to the inside forearm, then head cut. The opponent parries
either quarte or does not react to the feint.

With Combination of Point Thrust and Cutting Action

The feint starts with the point and the final action is a cut to the body
or forearm. Example: straight feint, then cut to the flank. The opponent
parries either quarte or prime.

The feint starts with a cutting motion and ends with a point action to the
body. Example: head feint, then disengage point to the body. The opponent
parries quarte.

With Point Action Only

The feint starts with a point motion and continues with another point
motion. Example: straight feint, then deceive a lateral parry with a disengage point; or deceive a counter sixte with a counter disengage.

Compound actions with the point only are not recommended for they
invite a counterattack. Point attacks to the forearm are not recommended
because they are barely visible to the judges and director of the bout.

In all compound attacks with a lunge, the feint should start slightly ahead
of the leading foot with the final hit accompanying the lunge. When an

Head feint and flank cut

advance-lunge is necessary, the feint should be maintained until the rear foot lands on the floor followed by the final action with the lunge.

When compound feints are used, a break in tempo increases the chances of success. For instance: head feint, flank feint, and chest cut with an advance-lunge. The attack can start with the first two feints executed swiftly while maintaining the flank feint until the back foot reaches the floor. Then the chest cut is executed with the lunge. Or, the head feint can be maintained until the back foot lands on the floor, and the flank feint and chest cut are executed with the lunge.

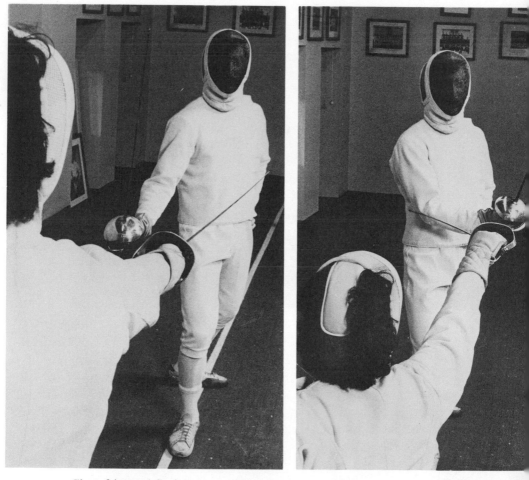

Chest feint and flank cut

With the same kind of attack using a lunge only, the same principle applies. The advance with a compound attack can be executed with a slow motion, a sliding step, or with a jump, then may be followed with a lunge or a fleche.

Classic Compound Attacks (including one feint)

Feint	Opponent's parry	Possible final action
Head feint	Quinte	Forearm cut Flank cut Belly or chest cut Disengage point
Flank feint	Tierce	Head cut Belly or chest cut Disengage point
Chest feint	Quarte or prime	Head cut Flank cut Forearm cut
Point feint	Quarte	Flank cut Head cut Disengage point
Point feint	Counter tierce	Counter disengage with the point

For classic compound attacks including two feints, the first two feints should aim at different targets and the final action hit on a different target from the one threatened by the second feint. Examples: head feint, flank feint, chest cut. Head feint, flank feint, head cut. The compound attacks with two feints require excellent technique in execution and perfect coordination of arm and legs.

Analysis

Tactical purpose and the distance from which the attack is launched require different uses of the feint. If it is to draw a defensive move immediately, the feint should not linger. Otherwise the blade may be caught by the opponent's defensive move. The attack in this case should be executed practically in one tempo (particularly useful at middle distance). The feint may also be used to fix the opponent's attention while gaining the proper distance for greater success in the final hit. In this case, the feint should be done smoothly to avoid too quick a defensive reaction by the opponent, and the final action of the attack should be executed at maximum speed or acceleration.

In the execution of compound attacks, blade control is essential while aiming at the target to achieve the proper effect (impression); to be able to deceive the opponent's defensive move; and to hit accurately on the intended target.

Speed in executing the compound attacks is certainly important. However, the control and use of speed with acceleration do more to set up the proper attack than a constant charging at the opponent, a flaw of many sabre fencers who cannot progress beyond the superficial aspect of fencing.

In the feint, the point should be accurately aimed at the target through finger action. The angle of the blade, depending on the distance between the two fencers, has an important bearing on provoking the opponent's reaction at the intended moment and with the expected defensive move.

The tendency to punch with the shoulder when feinting gives a whipping motion to the point, which makes the subsequent parry extremely easy for the opponent. It also delays execution of the next action, allowing the opponent time to reach a safe distance and permitting him to make a successful defensive move at the end of the attack.

The position of the guard and the front edge of the blade is important when making the feint. It should be able to block a counterattack (stop cut) to the forearm. The level of the feint and the arm necessary to provide protection depends on either the height of the opponent or the kind of counterattack he may prefer.

Finally, the fencer should make every feint move in a constant progression toward the target in order to emphasize the value of each feint.

Combination Parries

The less a fencer reacts to the opponent's feints the better chances he gets to parry the final strike of the oncoming attack. However, it is not always possible to maintain control of one's defensive reflexes against an opponent who uses a fast break of tempo in his compound attacks.

A very effective way to counteract such attacks is to use combination parries.

The combination parries consist of different hand positions at a slow pace, while keeping the right distance during the opponent's attack. These positions are not necessarily reactions to the opponent's feints but rather a way to close one line and subtly direct the opponent's attack into a line that will be blocked with the final parry.

Combination parries require smooth control of the tempo and the blade so that the final parry will not be delayed or fail to block sufficiently. They are effective because they deter the opponent from making deep feints, which require reaction and detract from smooth control of the tempo. Limiting the opponent's attack progression makes his final move much easier to anticipate and easier to parry. Sometimes a counterattack may be launched while the opponent proceeds with the attack and is convinced that he has you on the defensive.

Combination parries are usually more effectively used with the arm three-quarters extended, for they allow a greater distance of safety.

Examples of combination parries: from the tierce position; quarte and tierce; quarte and seconde; quarte and quinte, and so on.

ATTACKS ON THE BLADE

Although all attacks on the blade in foil could also be used in sabre, the distance separating the sabre fencers makes most of them impracticable. The beat is the most commonly used and the most effective when distance permits. It can be executed from and to a tierce, quarte, seconde, or quinte position, depending on the blade positions of the fencers. The beat of prime is not recommended, for it requires a wide blade motion to contact the opponent's blade, leaving a wide target (arm and flank) open.

The beat is executed with a sharp rotation of the wrist and a tightening of the fingers (mainly the last three) on the handle at the moment of blade contact. The wrist is turned so to place the edge in position to contact the opponent's blade. In some instances the beat can be done with the back edge —for example: from tierce to quarte—when the attack is directed to the right cheek, for example. In every case, however, the beat should be done with the blade edge against the middle part of the opponent's blade.

Depending on the fencers' blade position the beat can be *direct,* that is, when the blades are in the same line or in contact (such as tierce to tierce); or *semicircular,* when one blade is in the high line and the other in the low line or vice versa (such as tierce to seconde). Preceded with a change or a circular motion, it is called a change beat or counter beat. In this case both blades are either in a high line or a low line (such as counter beat in tierce).

Beat Quarte

This is the most commonly used attack on the blade. From tierce, it is executed by an inward rotation of the wrist (to present the edge of the blade toward the opponent's blade) accompanied by a sharp downward motion

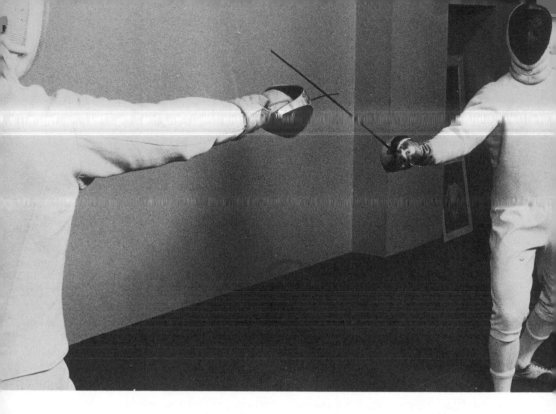

Beat on the blade and flank cut

that brings the blade down and against the middle part of the opponent's blade. At the same time, the fingers tighten on the handle to add sharpness in blocking the blade motion at the moment of impact.

Beat Tierce

This is done with a sharp outward rotation of the wrist and finger contraction on the handle. If begun from seconde position, it is executed with a semicircular motion.

Beat Seconde

If begun from tierce position, it is executed with a semicircular beat. If both blades are in second position, it is executed with a direct beat.

The beat is usually executed after the arm extension. When combined with an advance, the beat should occur at the moment the *rear* foot lands on the ground. When combined with a balestra, it should be when both feet land on the floor (that is, simultaneous with the jump).

Analysis

The purpose of the beat is to delay the opponent's defensive move. Depending on the tactical intent, the beat is executed with more or less intensity or sharpness to get the desired reaction. If the intent is to open the line for the succeeding attack, the beat should be very strong. However, if the intent is to provoke a specific defensive move on the part of the opponent (either a parry or counterattack), the beat is not used to try to knock the opponent's blade aside but rather is made with a softer impact.

Before using a beat attack, check the opponent's reaction; with some fencers the beat triggers an automatic riposte, particularly if done in the tierce position.

Usually it is essential to execute the succeeding attack without delay to avoid losing the right-of-way.

The beat can be deceived easily when the opponent telegraphs his intention or when he swings too widely in striking the blade. At the same time, be very careful in using a beat attack against a point-thrust feint with an extended arm. Often the intention behind this feint is to induce the beat with the intention of deceiving it.

Depending on the distance, a greater or lesser extension of the arm is necessary to make the beat.

COUNTERATTACKS

The counterattack is an offensive action executed against the opponent's attack. To be valid, the counterattack must either keep the opponent's attack from succeeding or hit one clear tempo ahead of the opponent's hit.

To reduce the opponent's attack, the counterattack is made with a point thrust that anticipates either an attack to the flank or a point-thrust attack. It is executed with a strong opposition from the guard and the blade and with the hand in a semi-seconde position. This counterattack requires perfect sense of distance, exact analysis of the opponent's attack, and perfect timing. The risk is that the slightest mistake in hand position may allow the opponent's attack to slip over the guard and reach the target.

To hit ahead of the opponent's hit, the counterattack can be executed either with a cutting action or a point thrust. With a cutting action it is called a *stop cut*. The stop cut is the current form of counterattack. It can be made either to the forearm or, more rarely, to the body; at the beginning of the opponent's attack or during its execution. The purpose is to hit one full tempo ahead of the opponent's hit.

The execution of the stop cut takes the same form as a simple attack to the forearm or body. The counterattack aims at the forearm when the opponent, making a feint or even a simple attack, leaves his forearm unprotected. The counterattack to other parts of the body target is justified when the opponent makes slow attacks or complex attacks involving too many tempos. The most favored counterattack in such cases is a stop cut to the head (to the flank, in some instances). The stop cut must be executed before the final motion of the opponent's attack.

If the opponent uses the beat attack too often, the aim is to deceive the beat by dropping the blade and cutting at the forearm (outside or under) immediately by a motion of the wrist.

Any stop cut to the forearm will be followed automatically by a fast retreat and a parry, either to help gain the "tempo ahead" over the opponent's hit or to eventually parry the finale of the opponent's action if the counterattack has failed.

When the stop cut is to the head, it helps to use a half-lunge to ensure reaching the target and also so that the sudden change of distance may stop the opponent's attack. However, against a simple direct attack, the stop cut to the body is automatically wrong, because of the right-of-way taken by the attack.

Stop cut, retreat, parry, and riposte

Counterattack with Point Thrust

This action is usually intended to hit the body and requires a half-lunge.

Defense against Counterattacks

Technique   The best defense against counterattacks is basically to give the opponent little opportunity to execute them. This can be done by developing perfect arm extension in executing both feints and attacks and by using the maximum coverage that the blade and guard can offer.

Tactical   Offensively, the best tactics against counterattacks are (1) to use mainly simple attacks to offset the validity of the counterattack; (2) to avoid using attacks that are too complex; and (3) to be prepared automatically to offset any counterattack. For instance: If the counterattack is expected on the outside forearm, rotating the wrist to the right at the moment of the opponent's counterattack will oppose one's guard and blade to the oncoming blow. (If the stop cut is intended for the inside forearm, rotating the wrist to the left will cover the target.) The original attacker then should proceed with the final move of the attack, which, depending on the distance, may be executed from the en-garde position or require either a lunge or a fleche.

The final move, in some instances, is a riposte if there is a definite break in tempo to block the counterattack. However, when there is no break in tempo and the opposition with one's guard and blade has negated the counterattack, the counterattack has "fallen on the blade," thus allowing one's attack to be valid. For instance: head cut feint with a quick wrist rotation at the time the counterattack is effected, continued with either a head cut or a belly cut, and so on. If the counterattack is not forthcoming, one's attack has the right-of-way and must be parried by the opponent.

Defensively, the best tactic against counterattack is second intention. The purpose of second intention is to use counter time, an offensive action that follows the parrying of a counterattack. The sequence is as follows: (1) preparation of the attack to induce a counterattack from the opponent, (2) parry of the counterattack, and (3) riposte immediately to any of the opponent's open targets. The preparation requires offensive intent to induce the opponent's counterattack. In most cases the feint must be combined with an advance or balestra. The correct distance and quick reaction with the parry will be the determining factors in the execution of a successful counter-time action. Because of the probability of an automatic, quick retreat by the opponent after executing his counterattack, the fencer must be prepared to execute the riposte with a fleche or a lunge.

As an example: quick chest feint or head feint with an advance; the opponent counterattacks with a point thrust; parry quarte and riposte to the belly or the head. If the opponent parries systematically after his counterattacks, a compound riposte is more appropriate.

Finta in Tempo

The finta in tempo in its execution is like a compound counterattack with a break of tempo. However, it is intended as a tactic for counteracting the opponent's "second-intention" action. The execution of the finta in tempo requires a perfect judgment of both the opponent's intention and reactions. When the fencer prepares to induce his opponent to counterattack, the opponent reacts with a false counterattack in order to provoke the parry and then deceives it with either a cut to the body or a point action.

VARIETY OF ATTACKS

Redoublement

As defined for the other weapons, the redoublement is a second attack that immediately follows an unsuccessful offensive action. It is preceded with a recovery either forward or backward. Because of the distance between sabre fencers, the redoublement has a tactical advantage and is the most-used of all three types of attacks.

The redoublement is particularly effective against fencers who parry without riposting and rely on distance for safety. If their defensive move is accompanied with an exaggerated backward lean, most likely they are unable to riposte or to execute another retreat.

The redoublement requires strong legs for the forward recovery and the succeeding lunge. During the recovery one should guard against a counterattack by the opponent. The arm should be kept extended and compound attacks should be used preferably for the second-offensive action.

The redoublement can be executed either with a lunge or a fleche. For example: head cut attack with a balestra, immediate recovery forward, followed with a head feint and cut to the flank with either lunge or fleche.

Reprise

The reprise is also a redoublement of attack but executed from the lunging position. It can be aimed at the forearm or the body, with either an indirect or a compound action.

The reprise, like the redoublement, is effective against an opponent who does not riposte immediately. It is best prepared if the first attack proceeds without triggering the opponent's defensive reflexes. This requires that the attack be done at a rather slow tempo, and the consecutive offensive action immediately and at full speed.

Remise

The remise is a second-offensive action executed against an opponent who either parries without riposting or delays his riposte too long. It is performed in the same line in which the parry has taken place. It can be aimed at the forearm or body and usually requires that the opponent leaves the line open after his parry. Because of the blade position in sabre, the remise requires perfect timing, distance, and judgment.

Remise to the body can be done after a fleche, from the lunging position or while recovering backward. There are very few opportunities to use remise during a bout because of the almost instinctive reaction to riposte at the first blade contact among sabre fencers. Often the remise tends to fuse with the counterattack. However, the execution of the remise should not be ignored.

Examples of when to use it: Against an opponent who parries quarte without riposting and automatically returning to tierce position, a remise to the chest or to the head is advisable. The same can be done against a fencer who parries quinte and does not riposte and return to his tierce position. If the delay while holding his quinte parry is sufficiently long, an immediate remise to the forearm is most effective. Otherwise the remise is aimed at the head as the opponent instinctively takes his tierce position.

Analysis

The variety of attacks requires that the opponent does not use the right-of-way immediately with the riposte or that he ripostes with either a delay or a compound action. The choice of using either one of the three variety of attacks depends mostly on the opponent's position and reaction at the time of his defensive move.

BOUTING

As in foil, the best way to score a hit is to surprise the opponent with a simple attack to any of the open targets. If the opponent is defending well, compound attacks are the next step.

The fencer should always be prepared to use his defensive moves and be ready to use the stop cut sometimes when his opponent's forearm target is uncovered.

In the beginning, particular attention should be given to distance, which is paramount to success. Footwork is important in the process, to maneuver the opponent to the distance of one's own attack and to surprise him with a swift offensive action.

Preparations include feints accompanied by advances, gliding steps, false attacks, and so on. These serve to check the opponent's actions and to discover his reactions.

During a bout the fencer must decide whether to attack or defend. The attack is the best way to score in sabre fencing and should be given priority, especially if one has successfully used it in a bout with a particular opponent. On the other hand, a good defensive game may be most appropriate when the opponent's attacks are easy to anticipate. The attack should not be stressed to the detriment of defensive development. Both are necessary for a successful game.

As right-of-way is involved in sabre fencing as in foil, the same three circumstances for a successful attack in foil are valid in sabre: (1) the right distance, (2) the choice of the right attack, (3) the choice of the right moment to attack. The decision as to when to attack will result from concentrating on catching the opponent unprepared or off balance. For example: when he drops his arm, or relaxes his guard position; when he makes preparations for his attack, such as feints, advances, etc.; when he recovers from an unsuccessful attack. The decision should be made only when the distance factor is favorable for the development of the attack.

Many fencers have difficulty parrying quinte or simply do not react to an attack to the head. Basically, quinte is a difficult parry to execute and if done incorrectly or at the wrong time, it is easy to deceive. The reluctance of many fencers to parry quinte may stem from the fact that it requires a wide movement, which leaves most of the target open—that is, the arm, flank, and chest. Its deception can be followed by an attack indiscriminately and almost instinctively to any of these open targets.

Consequently, it is recommended that a bout be started with an attack to the head. From such an attack, depending on the opponent's reactions, a strategy can be developed. This will include either the use of compound attacks if the opponent has reacted to the first attack with a defensive move; a counter riposte if the opponent has successfully parried and tried to riposte; a redoublement if the opponent has retreated out of reach with or without a parry; or a counter time if the opponent has made a counter-attack.

Sabre is a very aggressive game resulting from the necessity to attack the opponent to prevent attack. This is why at the command "Fence" sabre fencers very often attack simultaneously, thus provoking a double hit—which cancels out. On the other hand, a simultaneous action may be needed to uncover the opponent's reaction.

Often, however, the simultaneous action is a result of either stubbornness or insufficient strategic concept. Against this type of fencer it is advisable to use second intention after the first or second double hit. This will be based on timing, as one expects the opponent to attack immediately at the command "Fence." With this command, one should pretend to attack but instead revert to defense with a quick, simple parry, such as quinte or prime taken in a sweeping action at the very beginning of the opponent's attack and followed with an immediate riposte. This usually surprises and cautions the opponent about attacking again. The psychological result can then be used to make one's own attack at the next command of "Fence."

Against a fencer who reacts almost instinctively with parries to every feint, the compound attack should be executed at full speed and without delay. Against a fencer with good control of his reactions and of distance, the feints should be done at slower tempo and with deep penetration to induce him to parry. The deception should then occur at the very last moment as the opponent parries.

Against an opponent who uses stop cuts, counter time is the best tactic to employ. For instance: a deep feint to the head to induce the opponent to stop cut—then block the stop cut and follow by an attack either to the head or the chest. The counter time is executed practically without break of tempo, for the opponent must react at the very moment the feint begins to be in time. Counter time may require the use of the lunge, advance lunge, or fleche.

Defense

The basic defensive system in sabre, which includes three parries (tierce, quarte, and quinte), is simple to develop. However, its simplicity makes it somewhat vulnerable. To make the parry system more effective it should be combined with: footwork (usually the retreat); the right distance needed for blocking the opponent's attack when it reaches the end of its momentum; the minimum move required to use the right parry at the last moment to prevent the opponent from deceiving it; and finally, correct analysis of the opponent's attack.

Although the tierce position should be kept until the final parry must be taken, a too-rigid position can delay the final move until too late. It is recommended that combinations of parries be made during the opponent's preparation to create confusion about the kind of reaction he may expect.

If the opponent leaves his forearm open while executing his attacks, a quick stop cut followed by a fast retreat is then best. Timing the opponent's attack is necessary, for to be valid the counterattack must be delivered one full tempo ahead of the opponent's hit.

Combining counterattacks and defensive moves is very disturbing to an opponent. When this result is attained, the situation should be exploited by starting one's own attack based on previous observations of the opponent's reactions.

ELECTRICAL
APPARATUS

The electrical apparatus which is necessary in official competitions in foil and epee includes:

A scoring apparatus with extension lights

2 reels, one on each end of the strip

2 floor cables, connecting the reels (or spools) to the scoring machine.

A cable links the scoring machine to a source of current, which can be a house outlet or batteries. Finally, a metallic strip, made of copper or brass mesh, covers the surface on which the fencers move (that is, the strip). This metallic strip is grounded so that any hit made on it with either the electrical foil or epee point during a bout is neutralized and will not trigger the signal lamps on the machine.

Although an electrical machine can be bought for either weapon, modern technology has made it possible to manufacture a single unit which will serve both for foil and epee. A simple switch changes the circuit to either foil or epee, depending on the need. Attempts have been made to manufacture an electrical apparatus for sabre, but the technical problems to achieve a design that will allow scoring with either the point or the edge of the blade are very complex. At the present time, the most developed apparatus would require changes or modifications either of the valid target or of the sabre conventions.

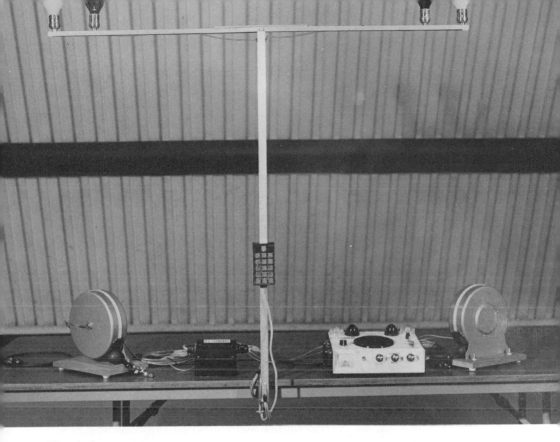

Electrical apparatus

The electric circuit used in foil is a "closed" circuit, while in epee it is an "open" circuit. Each cable involved in the different connections is made up of three wires, two of them for the circuit that allows either the "flowing" or the "cutting off" of the current, depending on the weapon. The third wire is intended to ground the metallic strip and the weapon in epee, while in foil the third wire of the body cord is clipped to the electrical jacket worn by the fencer.

The signal lamps are placed on top of the apparatus. The electrical machine, when specifically built for epee, requires two lights, one for each fencer's side (either green or red). When the light on the side of the fencer lights, it means that the fencer has been hit. If both lights light at the same time (both fencers score within 1/20th of a second), it is a double hit and a touch is counted against each fencer.

The foil machine requires four signal lights, two on each fencer's side (one white and one colored light). The white lights are connected to the off-target areas and the colored lights with the valid target. If both lights on the same side go on, the fencer has been hit off-target first and then on the valid target. Foil conventions decree that the off-target hit cancels the valid hit. If only the colored light is lit, the hit has landed first on the valid target. When this occurs, the circuit for the off-target light is automatically shut and possible subsequent hits on the off-target area cannot register on the machine. Therefore, the hit has to be allowed. However, when only the two colored lights are lit, the decision as to who benefits is made by the presiding director of the bout according to foil conventions and right-of-way.

Electrical Weapons

The electrical blade in foil and epee is mounted with an electric point which is connected through a thin wire in foil, and two thin wires in epee, going in a groove along the blade to a connector inside the guard.

A body cord made of a flexible, light cable (with three wires) runs up the fencer's arm under his jacket. One extremity is connected to the connector inside the guard while the other end is connected to an extensible cable mounted on a spring powered take-up reel located at the end of the side of the strip. The fencers, therefore, have total liberty of action on the strip as the cable inside the reels has a minimum length of 18 to 20 meters.

Needless to say, the electrical system used with the machine is 100 percent safe and does not offer any risk of injury to the fencers.

The fencers must provide their own weapons (a minimum of two usually being required), their own body cord (again two being necessary), and for foil their own metallic jacket.

LESSONS

In learning to fence, the beginner first encounters the purely physical aspects of fencing. In so doing, he develops conditioned reflexes.

Confronted with a point directed toward his chest, the beginner instinctively reacts by leaning backward or retreating rather than using his weapon to deflect the opponent's blade as would a trained fencer. Through constant repetition of precise movements, a fencer trains his reflexes to respond according to the momentary situation. This is accomplished through lessons first, then developed through practice. However, one should remember that repetition without thought can produce an overly mechanical approach. It is important, therefore, to remember the following principle: Any muscular effort is as much a mental act as conversation or writing. For example: If while lifting a heavy object one is distracted or undergoes an emotional reaction, the object may be dropped or the lifting stopped because the mental forces directed toward accomplishing this task have been diverted from controlling the action of the muscles.

If the object to be lifted is a light one, little concentration is required toward this effort, particularly if training has already taken place. Mental concentration may then be directed to other aspects of the activity.

In both the physical and intellectual aspects of human activity, mental concentration is required to attain optimum development. Fencing demands intense concentration, not because great strength is needed, but because the actions involved are complex and also because it requires, and helps to develop, associated mental qualities such as judgment in making decisions, determination in achieving a result (whether it be a touch or winning a bout), self-control in not giving into the opponent's attempt to disrupt one's game or concentration, and quick thinking in finding the right tactic.

Fencing as a sport is classified as a "finished skill" that requires both high speed and accuracy. Technique is defined as "the mechanical or formal part of an art." It allows the expression of one's potential at its highest level. Potential is determined by the quality of the fencer's senses, physical coordination, reflexes (both mental and physical), tactical ability, imagination, and so on. Undoubtedly, the foundation of a fencer begins with the development of his technique.

The teaching approach and manner of executing fencing actions have been replaced by a more natural expression. Effectiveness and scoring have become the main concern, without, however, abandoning the form and natural elegance proper to fencing.

The need to develop technique through training is as great today as it was in the past for one who wants to gain experience and attain championship level. The notable difference is that physical conditioning, which was once developed mainly through fencing lessons, is now achieved separately through calisthenics and physical exercises. This allows the fencing master and the fencer to concentrate on technique and concept during the entire lesson.

The advent of electrical foil was said to have produced a "revolution in fencing"—that is, that foil fencing had undergone important changes in its fundamental principles. This is not true. The form of Russian and Polish fencers, newcomers among the top fencers at the time the electrical foil came about, could not be closer to the classical form used by the Italian, French, or Hungarian champions of the past.

Although the heavier new weapons certainly influenced technique, the real revolution was the improvement of training methods in sports, the necessity to develop stamina to endure long and arduous competitions, and the ever-increasing number of major contenders for gold medals, particularly in the Olympic Games. Despite the improvement in training technique, it would be wrong to think that the principles established in the classical method of fencing must be changed. It is rather the true interpretation and the manner in which the principles are taught that need to be improved.

DEVELOPING TECHNIQUE

The development of technique requires regular practice, attention and concentration, and constant correction. A fencer is like an opera singer who needs lessons on a regular basis to improve or maintain his or her high standards of performance. Lessons have different purposes aiming at the different aspects of the development of technique, tactics, or training.

Learning fencing actions and their mechanics is accomplished through what we will call *academic* lessons. Learning the application of these actions (offensive and defensive) under various situations requires *bouting* lessons. Finally, learning to maintain or develop the rhythm, speed, and accuracy of specific actions under conditions similar to those of a bout necessitates *training* lessons.

The student should invariably precede the lesson first with a warmup of ten to twenty minutes. This will be attained through general calisthenics—that is, exercises concentrating on the arms, legs, and trunk of the body. Then there should be ten to fifteen minutes of special exercises related to fencing—for example: lunges combined with footwork.

Too many fencers tend to take their lessons without being prepared both physically and mentally. Very often one sees fencers sitting down for quite a while just waiting for their turn to take a lesson. The result is that often their muscles are unprepared to sustain the effort that the lesson requires. The consequence is either a loss of time for both the master and the student or the risk of a possible accident (by pulling a muscle, for instance). The negative aspect of taking lessons under such conditions should be particularly stressed at the very beginning so that students know from the start how to use with maximum results the time they spend in training or learning fencing.

The three kinds of lessons mentioned above should be given with a progression in the amount of effort to be spent by the pupil. The intensity of the lesson should build up to its maximum toward the end, then finish with a few minutes of easy actions to allow the student to unwind. Basically a lesson should include:

1. Simple to compound attacks as stretching exercises and some parries and ripostes, all at a slow or normal speed. The purpose is: to get the student adjusted to the distance of attack and the distance for ripostes, to make some correction concerning the execution of the actions, and to prepare the pupil for a greater effort.

2. Review of actions learned previously, or execution of some actions already known but done at a greater speed.

3. Learning of new actions.
1. Application of new actions.
5. Exercises aimed at blade control and point accuracy and/or unwinding exercises.

The length of the lesson will vary depending on the technical level of the student, his physical conditioning, and the purpose of the lesson. It may last from twenty to sixty minutes.

Reciprocals

A type of exercise that aims at developing mechanism and speed of execution is the *reciprocal*. It is extremely useful for both beginners and advanced fencers. It can be practiced before or after the lesson. The attack to be executed and the appropriate defensive move are established ahead of time. One fencer executes the attack while the other executes the parry (and riposte eventually) without retreating. In this exercise, the purpose is not to repeat the action but rather to concentrate on developing force with the action. This requires concentration by the fencer who does the attack. It necessitates checking on his en-garde position, balance, and relaxation, and preparedness of the muscles to transform energy into dynamic motion. Achieving speed and perfecting execution are the two elements involved in this exercise.

In the meantime, the defender sets himself up to be ready to parry the attack effectively while using his blade with the minimum energy. The exercise is repeated several times, then the partners reverse roles: the attacker becomes defender and vice versa.

It is important that the fencers execute the actions in an honest manner, keeping in mind that they are helping each other to improve mechanics, reflex, and speed. Distance between the fencers should be correct, neither too close nor too far. The defender should not retreat but should use blade action only. Any simple or compound attack, preceded or not with an attack on the blade, may be selected for the reciprocal exercise.

Academic Lesson

The academic lesson is basically the "learning" lesson. The technique of movement and the technique of execution are specifically stressed. This type of lesson aims at beginner and advanced fencers equally. Its purpose is to learn new actions or to improve on some already known, and its intent is to help fencers develop coordination between arms and leg speed and control of tempo.

To teach a new action requires demonstration of the action (one picture is worth a thousand words!). The action is divided into secondary movements, which the pupil will have to execute separately also. Secondary movements usually involve at the beginning (1) point motion, (2) arm extension, and (3) lunging action, any of which may or may not be combined with an advance. The motions should be executed first slowly, then the complete action at normal speed. Only when the student has gained sufficient mechanical control of the action should greater speed be demanded of him. The same procedure should be used when the advance-lunge is incorporated into the action.

Offensive actions should be executed first from the en-garde position; then with a lunge; then with an advance lunge. The fleche is not recommended at the beginning.

During the academic lesson special attention should be given to the en-garde position: balance, and shoulders relaxed; the holding of the weapon: hand in supination and without tightness. This is the best way to avoid shoulder action. The arm extension should be executed without locking the elbow, for this would hinder the fingers from performing as well as make it difficult to reverse blade action from offensive to defensive. While the arm is extended, constant check should be made of the position of the knees, which should be bent at all times. Standing up limits the action of the legs. Knees that are bent too deeply in a crouched position require an adjustment of the body's center of gravity in order to allow the legs to function with the maximum efficiency, speed, and proper projection.

The position of the feet at a right angle helps give the lunge its proper direction. If the leading foot is turned inward even slightly, the lunge will follow the same direction and impair the balance.

The lunge implies dynamic action of the back leg while the front foot is moved forward with the heel skimming the floor, and not in an up-and-down motion. At the end of the lunge check the balance and position of the trunk. The student should be able to keep the lunging position while the point is on the target without having to make any adjustment to keep his balance. During the advance-lunge, the balance and position of the knee at the end of the advance are important, for they determine the spontaneity and speed of the succeeding lunge.

Defense

The defensive reflex through blade motion is a totally learned response in a fencer. Therefore, the lesson aims (1) at getting the student familiar with and accustomed to the point of the blade coming toward him without his reacting with his body first, and (2) getting him to control his nerves so that his reaction becomes one of blade motion. Through constant practice the student learns to control the wideness of his arm motions and, subsequently, the blade and its point. Finally, the lesson helps develop the reflex of riposting after a successful parry.

Practice reduces sharply the time reaction of a pupil—that is, between the moment his eyes perceive the oncoming point and that when the brain transmits the command for action to the nerves and muscles of the arm. The development of a good defensive system involves the mechanical aspect of the different parries followed by the development of the defensive reflex.

To master the mechanical aspect, repetition of the defensive movements is required. These will be performed slowly at the beginning with emphasis on hand and blade position, and then faster in response to progressively rapid oncoming attacks. To develop good defensive reflexes, the pupil learns to parry at the last possible moment—when the point is only a few inches away from his chest instead of at the very beginning of the attack.

Parries should be learned from (1) the en-garde position, (2) with a retreat, (3) from the lunging position, and (4) after a recovery. The parry with an advance, which sometimes can be used tactically, should-be taught only when the fencer has reached a relatively advanced level of technique.

The execution of the riposte automatically follows the same progression as that used for the parry. A word of caution, however, concerning the riposte executed with a retreat: Too often fencers are trained to riposte automatically with a retreat. This is wrong; the riposte will fall short on most occasions. The only time the riposte will reach the target when executed with a retreat is when the opponent makes a continuation or a fleche. Once the attack has been parried, the riposte should follow while the opponent is at close range. Retreating with the riposte eliminates this opportunity and cancels the benefits of having successfully parried the opponent's attack. The decision to riposte with a retreat should be based on tactical considerations or on the question of distance rather than as an automatic action.

Blade position in the parry is extremely important; it determines the length of the trajectory the point must follow to reach the target and the ease with which the riposte will be carried out. A relaxed elbow at the moment of parrying allows the maximum speed and point control and facilitates the execution of the appropriate type of riposte.

To help the student develop good defensive reflexes, after a few lessons the teacher should execute some surprise attacks against the student—for example: while he is preparing his action or gaining the distance. The attack should be a simple parry at first, then the parries of a compound action. The same educative process should be used by the teacher parrying the student's attack occasionally and riposting or by attacking him when he recovers from the lunging position.

Bouting Lesson

The purpose of the bouting lesson is to train the fencer to execute offensive and defensive movements under conditions similar to a bout. Corrections are aimed not so much at the mechanical aspect of the actions as at (1) the distance to be kept during the lesson, (2) the distance from which the pupil can develop his attack and succeed, and (3) the moment at which to attack.

The attack will be specified and also the particular circumstances under which the student should start his attack. For instance, the student has to execute a one-two when the teacher makes a change of engagement. The role of the teacher is to create the bout conditions to allow the student to evaluate the opportunity without being distracted by other tactical elements at first. As the student progresses, the conditions are made more difficult, either by changing the rhythm or the complexity of the action or by combining the attacks with advance-lunge, the parries with advance or retreat, and, similarly, the ripostes.

In any event it is important that the student gain confidence in his ability to carry out the attack successfully or to defend himself effectively. When the student reaches an advanced level, he is given a choice of actions to be executed. For example: The teacher asks the pupil to execute a remise or reprise if his attack is parried and there is no riposte by the teacher, or otherwise to parry the riposte and execute the counter riposte.

The bouting lesson should not include more than three or four different actions, which would be too much to learn at one time, and also because execution requires great concentration by the student. Footwork is essential in maintaining the right distance and its first direct application is in the bouting lesson.

Training Lesson

The training lesson primarily helps to maintain the fencer's technical and physical condition. The fencer executes different kinds of actions under different circumstances, different tempos, and so on. He usually performs a greater number of actions (from six to eight) than in the previous two kinds of lessons. In some cases the actions are repetitive, in some cases tactical, and so on. It aims for variety, while requiring the maximum speed in execution.

In this lesson, the teacher emphasizes actions that will constitute the student's basic game and are based on his physical qualities, the development of his technique, and the reflexes and tactics he has assimilated. A few minutes' break between change of action is recommended to give the fencer time to recuperate after each intensive exercise.

Group Lesson

This kind of lesson is particularly useful in the beginning and when there are a large number of beginners. It is the best way to teach beginners the mechanical aspect of fencing moves (defensive and offensive) and also to teach a number of fencers at one time. Otherwise there is usually a waiting list for individual lessons.

I believe that the group lesson is somewhat more productive in the beginning than the individual lesson. It allows more repetitive actions under more realistic conditions. Also, through vocal commands given to the group, the students are disciplined to react at the proper time. This helps them to develop controlled reflexes.

The group lesson follows the same progression as the academic lesson. The warmup can take place collectively, then the fencers are paired up in formation in two lines—straight, semicircular, or circular, depending on the space available. The lesson proceeds as follows:

1. Demonstration of the action to be executed, first by the teacher, then by one of the students.

2. Explanation of the different secondary movements involved in the action: (a) point motion, (b) arm motion, (c) lunging action, and (d) recovery.

3. Execution of the action at the teacher's command.

4. Corrections by the teacher.

5. New execution, either by command or individually at the students' own pace.

The appropriate defensive move can be demonstrated after the first few attacks have been executed or simultaneously with the demonstration of the attack. At this time, the students should be aware of using the proper hand position for moving the blade at the correct angle while keeping the point from going out of line.

The riposte should not be taught too soon, for it might distract the attacker from executing the attack with the maximum lunge. The defenders, meanwhile, learn to develop the feel of the blade during the parry, using the strong part to contact the weak part of the opponent's oncoming blade. After a while, the roles are reversed with the attackers becoming defenders, and vice versa. In the beginning it is more important to require perfect execution than urge speed or effectiveness.

The progression in group lessons is from simple to compound attacks executed with the lunge first, then with advance-lunge. The defensive actions also proceed from simple to compound and follow the progression of the attacks.

It is suggested that at the beginning the defenders receive the attack on the chest without parrying so that the attacker learns to raise his hand and relax his fingers when the point reaches the target. This avoids hurting the partner, and the attacker learns to control shoulder movement and to maintain his balance with the lunge.

A word of caution about group lessons: Because of the number of students involved at one time and the closeness with which they work, the mask *must be worn* at all times. Similarly, the point of the foil *should be kept down toward the floor when not being used in an exercise or when the students are listening to explanations.* Fussing with the foil and threatening other fencers when masks are not worn should be strictly forbidden.

However, fencing is not a dangerous sport. Most accidents happen when students do not respect the safety rules. Otherwise, there is no wound inflicted that cannot be treated in most cases with a Band-Aid!

CONDITIONING

Getting into condition for any sport involves goals and the relationships of one's activities to these goals. Conditioning should include both mental and physical components. In fencing, there are specialized areas of preparation for the demands peculiar to the sport. Conditioning is inseparable from the technical preparation for fencing and must be coordinated with one's progress.

These are the overall goals of a proper conditioning program: 1. To develop endurance and general physical fitness to the level of a middle-distance runner. One should have staying power to compete for long periods of time with many interruptions. One also must maintain explosive capacity in order to function forcefully in the offensive movements required in competitive fencing.

2. To be able to make precise, accurate movements. This involves mental preparation through concentration and self-awareness. Drills must be aimed at developing the above capabilities, and one must engage in and practice combat. Proper muscle development is necessary to enter into active sport. Serious competitive fencing requires additional concurrent psychological preparation.

The fundamentals of conditioning are determined by the physiology of

180

the muscle. When a muscle works it utilizes oxygen. The oxygen used is made up of two components: (1) that which can be replaced immediately and is part of the so-called aerobic metabolism; and (2) that which takes time to replace, or the component of anaerobic metabolism associated with the breakdown of glycogen and the production of lactic acid. Studies have shown that the trained athlete has two changes in his muscles, which result in increased capacity for strengh and endurance. First, the muscles are developed and somewhat hypertrophied, which leads to greater muscle bulk and thus a larger volume of stored energy-producing materials within the muscle itself. Second, there is a marked increase in the number of capillaries (small blood vessels within the muscle) leading to a more efficient exchange of oxygen from the circulating blood to the muscle. This results in a much more rapid recovery of the aerobic (fast) energy supply.

A physical-conditioning program should involve the following:

1. Cardiovascular conditioning resulting in increased general capacity for physical output.

2. Fencing, which in itself leads to development of the specific muscle groups stressed in fencing.

3. Specific exercises designed to develop muscle groups that the individual fencer tends to neglect, either because of his preferred fencing style or because of previous habitual patterns of movement.

PREPARATION FOR ENDURANCE

The conditioning required in developing the cardiovascular capabilities necessary for all-out performances and the muscular strength necessary for forceful execution must be separated from technical preparation. Yet the two inevitably blend in a fully developed program. Since fencing requires many unusual positions which are not part of the common responses of our physical makeup, the fencer must "program" himself in such a way that he will, by reflex, make the correct movements in the most effective manner possible. Programming is begun in the lesson and worked on during practice. In developing strength and endurance, it is important not to mimic fencing movements but rather to work on the capacities involved. Attempting to execute technical exercises and precision movements when fatigued counteracts the development of good technique. General-conditioning exercises should be separated from the technical aspect of fencing.

Running is the most valuable exercise for a fencer for developing both cardiovascular responses and explosive maneuvers, and stamina. Wind sprints should be interspersed with distance running. Gradual lengthening of the overall distance of one to two miles of running at any conditioning session should be striven for, and five miles is desirable in preparing for top-level competition.

Specific exercise patterns can be useful. The Royal Canadian Air Force Exercises, requiring only eleven minutes a day for men and twelve a day for women, can help to attain all-around, good physical condition. One can start these exercises at a low level and progress as one's abilities and inclinations dictate. General-conditioning exercises may be done to the point of fatigue. However, for specific exercises involving fencing movements, *quality before quantity* and *precision before speed* should be stressed.

Mobility and Relaxation

All individuals are one of two different muscular types: simply put, relaxed people or tense people. Any athletic or training program must take this into account. Individuals who are very muscular tend to become tenser than is necessary for optimal performance in fencing and must learn to devote time to developing relaxed muscles. This not only will lead to increased performance but will also prevent the type of injury common to the tense person. For such individuals the program should emphasize stretching exercises to lengthen muscle extension.

Psychological Factors

Psychological preparation is necessary so that the fencer learns to relax under pressure and to concentrate his energies to achieve explosive reactions. Let us consider two individuals who may maintain the same posture but differ in the following respect: Where one has relaxed muscles on both sides of a joint the other has tensed muscles. The one who has both sets of muscles relaxed merely has to tighten one set to produce the desired movement. The one who has both sets tensed must first relax the opposing muscles before the desired movement can be started. This leads to a loss of speed and a jerkiness or irregularity in the movement. To summarize, in combat, the ultimate aim of conditioning is to achieve mobility and crisp actions *without prior tense muscles.*

There is a form of relaxed tension in which an individual is prepared to move and is not tense in any way. In effect, the tension is mental but has not transmitted itself to the muscles. This form of tension or mental alertness is the desired state to achieve. It can be acquired only through concentration and practice. One way is to simply go limp while maintaining posture and being ready to move rapidly. This relaxation, once consciously learned, becomes almost unconscious and leads to the lightninglike reflex responses in parry-ripostes and in reacting appropriately to a defensive or offensive situation as it arises. In a situation where one must maintain a posture by keeping all muscles tense, a writer's cramp, in effect, can result. Those who tend to be tense may find that such cramps occur frequently and destroy their enjoyment of competition. If you do encounter this kind of problem, recognize what it is. A muscle has been kept tense for long periods of time. This minimizes its blood supply and, because of increased pressure, makes it work without productive effort. One should learn to relax when the opponent is out of distance and relative safety is achieved. Keeping flexible by extending, recovering, or making counters or simple movements is sometimes helpful. However, a definite program for learning to relax is a far more effective method of avoiding cramps.

PREPARATION FOR STRENGTH

Fencing is an inherently asymmetric sport. The rear leg and the front leg receive different stimuli. The hand holding the weapon and the hand in the rear have different functions. This can result in a disproportionate development of the stressed portions of the anatomy unless a general exercise program with symmetrical exercises is undertaken to develop the strength of both sides equally.

Strength, however, does not mean big muscles. The overly hypertrophied muscles of the weight lifter, particularly in the arm, are disadvantageous in fencing. Any program of physical training should avoid the types of exercises that lead to bulky muscles. Rather it should stress strength along with the capacity for rapid motion and flexibility.

Strong, adequate musculature leads to good balance and balance is the key to mobility in fencing. One must first begin with the legs. The quadriceps muscles and the long hamstrings need particular attention. A torn hamstring is a major injury. Prevention involves keeping the hamstrings relaxed and doing stretching exercises. Situps and stretching using the "hurdler's stretch" are mandatory. At best the fencer should be able to do a "split" and to control the movement into a split. The most dangerous situation is at the end of the lunge when the forward foot may not land properly or may slip. This can result in the foot sliding forward with a forced split, which can put the athlete out of action for many months. To learn the split, one should gradually stretch the hamstrings, using auxiliary support and pushing just a little bit further each day. It may take from six months to a year to perfect this. However, the security of being able to withstand this degree of stretching is worth the effort.

The quadriceps muscles play an important part at the end of the lunge. The quadriceps of the forward leg slow down the body, bring it to a stop, and provide the major effort for the recovery and return to the en-garde position. The quadriceps of the rear leg are essential to maintain the proper en-garde position. One of the earliest signs of fatigue in a fencer is the tendency to extend the rear leg, thus causing the fencer to lean forward to to stand up while in en-garde. This reduces mobility and the fluidity of movement.

The quadriceps of the rear leg tend to be less well developed. Strength in the rear leg requires exercises specifically aimed at the quadriceps. The simplest of these is to use weights that can be looped over the ankle and that will not cause discomfort when heavier weights are used. The exercise is performed by sitting on a table or other hard surface for support, hanging the legs from the knees, and making two movements. The first is to straighten the knee without lifting the thigh from the supporting seat, holding the position of straightened knee for six seconds, then releasing. This exercise should be performed in sets of ten to twenty-five repetitions of four sets, with a short rest between sets. The average individual should be able to lift 10 percent of his body weight; a trained athlete up to 25 percent of his body weight. One should start with a small number of weights, three to five pounds, then increase gradually as the exercise becomes easy to do.

The second exercise for quadriceps is to again hang the weights from the ankle, sitting so that the weights are swinging free from the floor, and to lift one's thigh from between three to four inches from the supporting surface without straightening the knee, hold the position for three to five seconds, and then return to rest. This again should be performed in sets of ten to twenty-five repetitions for a series of four sets. Equal development of the quadriceps will lead to an easier attainment of the proper en-garde position and the capacity to maintain it for longer periods.

With respect to the arms, it is important to develop a strong biceps and forearm muscles. The aim is not to lift large numbers of weights to develop a bulky musculature but rather to take a small weight that can be handled easily and to do repetitive exercises. One of the injuries common to fencers who parry incorrectly is the fencer's equivalent of tennis elbow. This occurs when rotatory movements are attempted against firm opposition, thus tearing the muscles of the forearm and in the the wrist. This can be minimized through a proper development of parries and strengthening the muscles to withstand the stresses encountered in fencing.

Useful exercises to prevent "fencer's elbow" are performed with weights from two to five pounds. The forearm is placed on a support (books will do), with the wrist and adjacent forearm unsupported. The forearm is rotated with the weights starting from a pronated position (palm down) and the wrist is extended starting from the same position. The forearm and wrist should be held in the first position for four to six seconds, analogous to the leg exercises described previously. Sets of ten to twenty-five repetitions in groups of three to four sets are advised.

COORDINATION AND MOBILITY

Fencing requires the control and suppression of certain movement patterns that are part of our normal activities. For example: as the left leg goes forward, the right arm swings forward; and as the right leg goes forward, the left arm swings forward and the right arm backward, and so on. The problem which the fencer faces is to dissociate his arm movements from his leg movements so that he can execute advances, retreats, balestras, lunges, and the like while his fencing arm remains loose, relaxed, and capable of executing movements that are not necessarily synchronous with those of his legs.

In learning complicated attacks and attacks with a preparation, the fencer must consciously emphasize his self-awareness of the dissociation of these movements. The natural development of techniques will lead to the loss of conscious awareness after the individual patterns have been learned so that the execution under practice and bout conditions eventually becomes second nature.

Alternative Sports

One of the problems a fencer faces in getting into proper condition is boredom with the same routine. Variety can be achieved through alternate sports that require similar mental and physical reactions. In particular, two sports have great value. One is basketball, particularly one-on-one play, which requires following one's opponent and reacting to his feints and deceptive movements in defense and feinting and gaining the extra step in offense. Observation of one's opponent is important here. Table tennis is another useful sport for the fencer in that it stresses fast reflexes along with delicacy of touch and capacity to mask one's intent in terms of offense and defense, all of which are part of fencing.

The proper use of alternate sports in a training program can help make what can be a dull routine into something that is fun.

Injuries

Prevention of injuries is one of the main effects of good conditioning. Sprains and muscle tears are the major problems that a fencer faces. Cramps have been discussed previously. One cannot stress enough that they are the result of a failure to relax in conjunction with the consequences of poor technique. Cramps are entirely preventable. The only other cause of cramps, aside from tension, is salt depletion in the body. This will occur when fencing in a warm environment, as in summer. Under these conditions the fencer should maintain his salt/fluid balance with appropriate balanced salt solutions commercially available—along with various "soft drinks."

A CONDITIONING PROGRAM

Drills and lessons should be performed when the fencer is warmed up, but not fatigued. If he is fatigued, he will tend to compensate for his tired muscles by making inappropriate movements. Once the movements have been learned—that is, proper conditioning has been effected and the fencer is programmed to perform the movements properly—he is ready to use these maneuvers under bout conditions and when fatigued, secure that he does not have to think about making the proper movement.

Sticking to a program is important. A different training schedule is necessary early in the season, in midseason, and at the peak of the season as one moves toward local and national championships. General conditioning, cardiovascular training, and muscle and strength training should take place early in the season along with basic technical development. In midseason, combative attitudes and technical problems should be stressed, while maintaining a proper exercise schedule that will sustain cardiovascular and muscular conditioning. At the peak portion of the season, bouting and combative situations should be stressed. A proper program suited to the individual's needs should be worked out and followed.

In general, principles for conditioning are as follows, with the understanding that the amount of exercise will depend on the physical condition and qualities of the individual.

Short sprints will develop speed; distance running will develop endurance. In the beginning one should jog a quarter of a mile, walk a quarter of a mile, then jog, for a total of two miles. This four-day-a-week program should be continued for approximately three to four weeks. One should then add calisthenics on a daily basis. Calisthenics will be described later in this chapter.

In the second month of training one should be jogging one-half mile, walking one-half mile, for a total of two miles. Wind sprints for a distance of one mile should be instituted two times a week, starting from a jogging speed, sprinting as rapidly as possible for twenty to thirty yards, slowing down to jogging pace, and then accelerating again. In the third month one should be working five or six days a week. The program should consist of daily exercises, wind sprints for one to one and a half miles, and being able to run a mile in six minutes.

Jumping rope is a fine way to begin any exercise program. Jumping rope should be done for approximately ten to fifteen minutes. It develops timing, coordination, and at the same time continuous cardiovascular conditioning.

Flexibility exercises and stretching exercises go together. Each of these exercises should be executed every day. The variety of exercises will prevent the program from becoming boring. It is important to set up the program in writing, establish a daily schedule, and then continue to perform it on a regular basis. An exercise program such as the Royal Canadian Air Force Program, described earlier, may be substituted for these.

Calisthenic Exercises

Pushups Position: lie flat on the stomach, hands flat on the ground under the shoulders, toes placed so as to provide support. Make the pushup hard enough so that you leave the ground, clap hands, and return them to position without allowing the body to contact the ground. If you cannot do this, starting from the same position, push up until arms are fully extended, maintain for a count of three, and bring body back to the ground without actually touching the ground. This should be repeated for a minimum of ten times and extending one's capabilities every week until one reaches a total of twenty repetitions per set. Once one has been able to do this, start executing the pushup with the clap at the ten-times level, and increase every week.

Situps These should follow the same daily routine of fifteen situps minimum, with increases every week.

Flexibility Exercises 1. Stand with feet apart, hands over the head, touching, arms straight at the elbows. Bend laterally toward one side as low as possible. Repeat on the opposite side and return to the original position. This cycle should be repeated ten times.

2. Stand with feet apart, hands clasped behind head, shoulders and elbows pulled back. Bend forward as far as you can, rotate your body toward the right side and return to the upright position. Repeat bending to the left

side and returning to the upright position. Do in sets of fifteen times.

3. Stand erect at attention. Bend forward without bending the knees, touch your toes, return to the upright position. Repeat ten to twenty times. As times goes on, one should be able to extend the bending, touching the toes with a clenched fist, and finally touching the palms to the floor.

4. Sit in the hurdle position with the right leg forward, bend your body forward, touch the right foot with both hands. Do *not* grab the foot and pull toward you, simply touch it. Repeat this ten times. Then repeat with the left in the reverse position ten times.

5. Lie on the ground, bring your trunk and legs up vertical with your shoulders and elbows on the ground and your hands supporting your hips. A three-point base will be formed by your shoulders and neck as one point and each elbow as the other two points. Make a bycicle-riding motion as fast as possible for a count of twenty, reverse for a count of twenty. Repeat the cycle twice.

6. Lie flat on back, arms extended sideways and legs straight out: without bending the knee, raise one leg perpendicular to the ground and swing it over to touch the opposite outstretched arm. Swing the back leg up to a vertical position and back to starting position. Repeat with the opposite leg to the opposite side. Repeat for a count of ten for each leg.

7. Lie flat on the back with the hands under the hips, legs straight together, toes extended. Raise the legs slowly without bending the knees for a slow count of ten until the legs are perpendicular to the floor. Lower the legs slowly and stop halfway, spread the legs, bring them together, then lower to just before touching the ground. Repeat raising, spreading, and bringing legs together ten times. Then lower to floor. The entire exercise should be repeated five times.

8. While lying on the ground, legs extended, bend one leg at the knee. With hands holding the knee, pull the leg against the chest, bounce three to five times, extend leg, and return to original position. Repeat with the opposite leg. This should be done for a total of fifteen times for each leg.

9. Stand at attention, keeping the heels together, squat and place hands on ground beside the feet, thrust both legs backward so that the weight of the body is supported on the hands and toes, return to squat position, then to vertical position. This should be repeated ten times.

10. Assume the position of a completed pushup. Bring the right knee up to the chest, leaving the left leg extended backward with the knee straight.

Extend the right leg backward and bring the left knee to the chest. This is to be done with a rapid rhythm for thirty counts.

Weight Lifting

Weight lifting must not be carried to any extreme. The aim in training for fencing is not to build muscle mass. One should use moderate weights in repetitive exercises rather than attempting progressively heavier weight values. If a muscle is weak, one should use heavier and heavier weights, but only with the advice of a coach or trainer. Weight exercises should develop endurance. This means that five- or ten-pound weights should never be exceeded with arm exercises; and when one wishes to increase the exercise load, one should increase the number of times the exercise is performed. If you have not lifted weights before, it is wise to start with small dumbbells of one and a half or two pounds and progress slowly. When you increase the weight, cut back on the number of times that you perform the exercise.

Weight-Lifting Exercises with Dumbbells   1. With hands at the side, holding dumbbells, raise both arms simultaneously until they are extended laterally. Hold for a count of four and return to the original position. Repeat ten times; increase daily by one repetition until twenty repetitions is reached. Then increase the weight by one pound. A maximum of five to ten pounds for a person of sixteen or seventeen years of age is sufficient.

2. Starting with the hands at the sides, raise the arms forward until they are straight out in front, then lower.

3. Starting with hands palms forward, flex elbows, bringing forearm to a vertical position, then slowly return to the original position. Repeat ten times, increase to twenty and do not exceed twenty.

4. Standing at attention, holding the dumbbells with the arms flexed, hands in supination and at shoulder level, extend the arm forward, holding the dumbbells away from body with arm at right angles from body. Return to a flexed-elbow position with the dumbbells at shoulder level. This should be repeated ten times.